Hezekiah Butterworth

**Up from the Cape**

A Plea for Republican Simplicity

Hezekiah Butterworth

**Up from the Cape**
*A Plea for Republican Simplicity*

ISBN/EAN: 9783744664912

Printed in Europe, USA, Canada, Australia, Japan

Cover: Foto ©ninafisch / pixelio.de

More available books at **www.hansebooks.com**

AUNT DESIRE COMES UP FROM THE CAPE.

*A Plea for Republican Simplicity.*

"If, with fancy unfurled
 You leave your abode,
 You may go round the world
 By the old Marlboro road."

THOREAU.

BOSTON:

ESTES AND LAURIAT, PUBLISHERS,

301-305 WASHINGTON STREET.

1883.

*Copyright, 1883,*
BY ESTES AND LAURIAT.

UNIVERSITY PRESS:
JOHN WILSON AND SON, CAMBRIDGE.

# PREFACE.

Why?

I was asked to attempt to write a light book for summer reading.

What?

I believe much in the New England of the past: in its principles, moral and political: I am acquainted with the farm house of the coast towns: I love it and respect its intelligent simplicity. It seems to me like a crown : it holds the best life.

Could I picture a family who maintain the early traditions of the country, and contrast it with one influenced by the haste for wealth, the feverish excitements of society, and the passion for display, of modern city life?

There rose before me good Uncle Eben, and quaint Aunt Desire, of the Cape.

Could I gather up all the old stories of their

farm house on the Cape, and make of them a picture?

Could I show how the present tendencies of city life appear to the eyes of one trained in the republican school of thought of half a century ago? I could try.

You have these pictures discursively and imperfectly drawn between intervals of work at an editor's desk. They are not exaggerated. Almost every incident, however strange any of them may seem, is but the reproduction of a fact from the note book of memory.

The lessons are simply the old ones: That work and contentment are the sources of happiness and that a true life is the best in its social and political results.

# CONTENTS.

### CHAPTER I.
Myself . . . . . . . . . . . . . . . . 9

### CHAPTER II.
In which Aunt Desire Constructs a Model Family Tree . . . . . . . . . . . . . . . . 15

### CHAPTER III.
Mrs. Desire Endicott Decides to Come up from the Cape . . . . . . . . . . . . . . . . 27

### CHAPTER IV.
Eben Favors Desire's Plans and Entertains Carrie with his Youthful Recollections of Mrs. Green . 37

### CHAPTER V.
The Old Orchard and Burying-Ground . . . . . 51

### CHAPTER VI.
Aunt Expresses her Opinion of Sister Carrie's Beau . 66

### CHAPTER VII.
I Receive a Strange Letter from Father . . . . 71

## CHAPTER VIII.

The Clam-Bake, and Story-Telling under the Trees . 75

## CHAPTER IX.

Carrie's "Boston" Story — "Dot." . . . . . . . . . 87

## CHAPTER X.

Rev. Mr. Glass makes a Clam-Bake for his City Friends with Results Described by Aunt to Uncle 104

## CHAPTER XI.

The Old House and Home, and Aunt Desire's Two Wishes . . . . . . . . . . . . . . . . . 110

## CHAPTER XII.

The Old Camp-Meeting and the New . . . . . . . 119

## CHAPTER XIII.

Picnics—"Crows in the Trees and Hawks in the Air," 125

## CHAPTER XIV.

Two Letters . . . . . . . . . . . . . . . . . . . 134

## CHAPTER XV.

Aunt's Farewell Exhortation . . . . . . . . . . . 139

## CHAPTER XVI.

Up from the Cape — A Walk — Aunt Calls on the Doctors . . . . . . . . . . . . . . . . . 148

## CHAPTER XVII.

Desire Calls upon Sundry Editors and Introduces to them the Pastoral Poems of Miss Flora Pink . 156

## CHAPTER XVIII.

November . . . . . . . . . . . . . . . . 167

## CHAPTER XIX.

Eugene Returns from Etretat . . . . . . . . . 173

## CHAPTER XX.

Aunt Relates to Uncle her luminous Conversation with Mr. McBride, the Agnostic . . . . . . . 185

## CHAPTER XXI.

"Up and down the Harbor goes the Henry Morrison"—Uncle's Narrative . . . . . . . . . . 191

## CHAPTER XXII.

Intelligence from Treasure Mountain . . . . . . 201

## CHAPTER XXIII.

The Black Sea—Uncle Eben's Narrative continued, 206

## CHAPTER XXIV.

The Clio Club—Aunt's Narrative . . . . . . . 213

## CHAPTER XXV.

Election Day . . . . . . . . . . . . . . . 222

## CHAPTER XXVI.

The Lectureship—Snow . . . . . . . . . . . 230

## CHAPTER XXVII.

December . . . . . . . . . . . . . . . . 238

## CHAPTER XXVIII.

AUNT DESIRE HEARS FROM THE WEST . . . . 241

## CHAPTER XXIX.

MAY — THE PRESIDENT'S LEVEE — LIFE LIES FAIR BEFORE ME . . . . . . . . . . . . . . . 245

## LIST OF ILLUSTRATIONS.

| | |
|---|---|
| Aunt Desire Comes up from the Cape, | *Frontis.* |
| Aunt Desire and Jeff | 18 |
| The Barn Theatricals | 49 |
| A Cape Clam-Bake | 75 |
| "Look Aloft" | 85 |
| Hoggarty Runs | 106 |
| "That is all Busted up" | 204 |
| At the President's Reception | 205 |

# UP FROM THE CAPE.

## CHAPTER I.

### MYSELF.

I had just graduated from the Latin School.

It was July, and the house was to be closed. Father and mother were going to the Hotel Wellesley for the rest of the summer. This was arranged for father's sake. He must be in Boston daily, and at work. Money must be made, else how were all the expenses of a house on the Back Bay to be met? It did not seem quite right — there was always a summer rest for each member of the family but for father.

Father was forty-two years of age. He was gray. There was a care-worn look on his face always. He constantly talked of investments and stocks; he was always in a state of feverish anxiety. He seemed to have no time for recreation, little for thinking on the subjects of life outside of his business, and as little for the enjoyment of nature and the pleasures that come from the cultivation of spiritual thought and life.

I ventured to say to him one day:

"Uncle Eben, who lives on the Cape, is sixty-five years old, and yet you look older than he."

"Eben never had any ambition. He is more contented with ten thousand dollars than I am with one hundred thousand dollars. He just reads religious books, goes to church, and roams about the woods and pastures like a cow-boy."

"But he seems happy. He is very intelligent, and has good health. He looks like a young man, and I wish you had less care and did not grow old so fast."

"It can't be helped; it can't be helped. It is our American life, my boy. It did not use to be so, when the country was new and people were more independent and democratic; but things have changed. Life is a fever. Your Uncle Eben may be wiser than I, after all, but I am launched on a rushing stream, and I must go on with the tide."

I was touched at this frank confession. One of my older brothers was studying abroad; another was idling at Newport; their expensive habits were compelling father to be more ambitious in his business schemes, increasing his anxieties and the number of his gray hairs.

My sister Carrie came into the room where we were sitting — father and I — and said:

"Jeff, have you decided where you will take your vacation?"

"Yes, partly; so far as this. I shall go where it will make father as little expense as possible."

"Jeff, you are a noble boy," said father.

"Thank you." I saw tears in his eyes.

"Carrie, let us go down on the Cape, and spend July and August with Uncle Eben and Aunt Desire."

"Agreed, Jeff. I always liked Uncle Eben — and Aunt Desire — well, she is a character."

"I am sick of all this straining after show and effect; all this slavery to stylish living; all of this aping Europeans in dress, politics, religion, music and art, and I would like to spend a few weeks in a home of true republican simplicity."

"Why, Jeff!" said father, the faint light of a smile overspreading his features. "How in the world, in the present state of society, did such a thought ever come to you?"

"For whom did you name me?"

"For whom? Why, Jefferson, Thomas Jefferson."

"So I have been told. I have been reading the life of Thomas Jefferson, and I think it would be a right good plan for American society to return to his simple, democratic principles. I am sick of snobs and second-hand Americans. Uncle Eben agrees with me. Won't we have a good time talking politics and telling stories under the trees,— Uncle Eben, Carrie and I?"

"And your Aunt Desire? Don't forget her," said father, laughing, and dropping the *Stock Reporter* into his lap. "Yes, your Uncle Eben can talk, and what he don't know about everything your Aunt Desire can tell him. Yes, yes; his home is one of 'true republican simplicity.' Glad you're going, Jeff. And you, Carrie. You certainly will have all of my good wishes."

And so it was decided that we should go down to the old family home, Carrie and I. We would study local history with Uncle Eben; we would get Aunt Desire to relate to us the old-time stories of provincial days. Uncle Eben was a famous story teller, too, but rather historical and heavy. For a story spiced with point and provincialism, I have known no equal to Aunt Desire.

Then, when the August days began to mellow

towards fall, we would go to the historic camp meeting at the Vineyard.

Uncle Eben himself was a Methodist; a broad one. The reading of Swedenborg, Emerson, and some of the best books of modern science had widened his mental horizon to such an extent as to make Aunt Desire tremble for his orthodoxy. But when Uncle Eben was a boy, the good orthodox people of the town had compelled the Methodists to pay taxes to help support their church. The Methodists protested; represented themselves as a persecuted people, and *grew*. At last they quite outnumbered their orthodox brethren, and then, acting upon the latter's own rule, they voted them out of the church and took possession of it. Eben being a Jeffersonian Democrat in politics, sympathized with the Methodists in their struggle against "taxation without representation," and united with them. Aunt Desire was a Methodist pure and simple, and had not been influenced by politics in her religious views. She used to declare in class meetings that she "never yet feared the face of clay," and our story will show that she continued in the same resolute state of mind after youthful curls had given place to cap borders. But Desire Endicott at heart was a very good woman.

As for myself, I was in danger of following my brothers into purposeless, pleasure-seeking habits of life. My chief amusement was billiards, and this was leading me at chance times, with certain agreeable but profitless companions, to the bar. A reading of the life of Thomas Jefferson, on account of my name, had somewhat interested me in the early principles and simple habits of American society a century ago. This experience had given me a certain respect for Uncle Eben's primitive opinions and manner of living, and had made pleasant to my imagination a long summer vacation on the Cape.

# CHAPTER II.

## IN WHICH AUNT DESIRE CONSTRUCTS A MODEL FAMILY TREE.

"Aunt Desire," as every one called her, was not an ignorant woman, as I found out, to my surprise, before I had spent a week at the old house. She used provincialisms freely, and Cape adjectives and expressions of surprise, and sometimes omitted the final "g" in her participles; but on most subjects to which she "had given her mind," she was remarkably well informed.

That she overrated the value of things of which she had read but not seen, was true; more cultivated people have done the same thing. That she regarded Boston much as the kitchen-girl looks upon Rome, and anticipated a visit to that city much as the old palmer dreamed of his pilgrimage, are also true. What wonder! Had she not read the Boston *Journal*, *Advertiser* or *Transcript* daily for twenty years, and a religious Boston paper for even a longer period?

My first discoveries of Aunt Desire's goodly stock of intelligence were hardly pleasant experiences. I happened to say, carelessly, one day, that I seldom attended the missionary concert in "our" church; that I was not much interested in foreign missions; and added the not very original remark, that "there were heathen enough at home," especially if one's home was in Boston.

She was making blackberry pies — how delicious these pies were, and how delightful their memory is yet! — when I volunteered the aforesaid remarks about foreign missions and Boston's heathen. She took her hands out of the dough, and turned around in a most awe-inspiring way, with a look of mingled pain and compassion in her face.

"Can I believe my own ears?" she said. "And you a *Boston* young man, too! Where the Woman's Board meets, too!"

I waited for a *third* rebuke, but she only looked at me for a time, her black eyes snapping.

Then, seizing the rolling-pin and lifting it aloft, she proceeded to free her mind in such a way that I sat transfixed with amazement.

"Heathen enough at home! Suppose St. Paul, the great Apostle to the Gentiles, had said *that!*

Why, the gospel would never have gone out of Jerusalem! If St. Augustine had said *that*, he never would have gone to preach in England, and *you* might have been a heathen to-day! Did you know that *your* ancestors were heathen, wanderin' about in sheep-skins, and that they were converted by *foreign* missionaries? Do you know that the missionary movement is the march of the church towards the millenium?

"If there is anything that makes Desire Endicott indignant clear through and through it is to hear some *reconstructed* Gentile like you; some descendant of a barbarian nation, like the bloody old Saxons from which nation *you* sprung, some narrow-minded, purse-puckered, empty-headed ignoramus like — well, not *you* this time, — like Deacon Bamp, for instance, speakin' lightly about the spread of the Gospel, and makin' an excuse for a want of generosity by talkin' about the heathen at home! Bless my soul, if the heathen at home were to be left to such people for help and enlightenment they would perish beyond any hope of recovery! Not that I mean to say that *you* are not generous, but it is plain to be seen that you have not been brought up right."

"I have not found time to read much upon the

subject, Aunt Desire; perhaps I ought to be better informed."

"Did you ever find time to read novels and such?" continued Aunt Desire, exasperatingly.

"A few."

"Don't you ever read the *Missionary Herald* and *Life and Light?*"

"Mother subscribes for them," I added. "I always put ten cents into the missionary box," and I thought I had now made my peace.

"Ten cents!" Up went the rolling pin. "Ten cents! Well, well, be charitable. Ten-cent pieces were made on purpose. Why, Jefferson Endicott, *I* give $20 a year to the American Board and $5 to the Woman's Board, and I save the money out of the profits I make by sellin' eggs, and I've always done my whole duty by the heathen at home. Nobody never asked Desire Endicott for anything that was good for them, that she could give, that they didn't get it. You ask the neighbors if it isn't so.

"You will find in my room the lives of Wm. Carey, and Dr. Judson, and Harriet Newell, and *all* the Mrs. Judsons, and the reports of all the different societies for the last ten years. When you feel lonesome, boy, you are free to go and get

AUNT DESIRE AND JEFF.

them. I hope I have n't offended you, nor nothin'. If I have, I beg your pardon. The fact is there's nothin' you could have said that would have so riled up the old Adam in me as just *that!*"

A short time after receiving this indignant protest and its apologies I happened to pass the open door of Aunt Desire's room. I glanced at her library of missionary literature, every book of which she had more than once read, and I felt sure that she knew vastly more than I about the religious progress of the world, and I mentally resolved to put twenty-five cents into the contribution box at any future missionary meetings I might attend.

The episode gave me a view of Aunt Desire's heart and character. She was wonderfully well read on certain subjects, and carried conviction with the expression of her opinions; while on other subjects her lack of information was as remarkable. I found this to be characteristic of many of the wives of the old Barnstable county farmers: they were clear in judgment, strong in conviction, and undeviating in principle; but their intelligence was directed to one thing. In many cases that one thing was church history. One woman that I met was perfectly familiar with Edwards' theological works; another with the lives of English Wesleyan preachers, such as Whitefield, Nelson, Fletcher of Madeley; another could recite all of Dr. Watts' hymns; another was a student of Neander and d'Aubigne. All were firm believers in republican equality and missionary movements. On thinking over the matter, I cannot see why this intelligence may not be as useful to the world in its results as the æsthetic studies and attainments of their young Boston sisters. In fact, I came to have a very deep respect for it.

They were model housekeepers, and never intrusted the fine art of cooking to some newly-arrived Bridget from the Green Island, where viands are not plenty, and where Mrs. Parloa does not hold schools. They regarded cooking, like the care of their children, as one of the trusts of home. All this was different from the experiences of the homes I had been accustomed to visit, and I must say increased my regard for the wholesome lives of the sturdy dames of Barnstable.

The house was old, but well-preserved and roomy. Aunt Desire's housekeeping was as perfect as the art can be made. Everything in the house was simple, though the furniture had an old-time elegance, but so arranged as to have an air of comfort.

"Yes," said Uncle Eben to me, one day, "Desire is a good housekeeper, but her intelligence is like the handle of a jug, all on one side. She has a sharp tongue; look out, my boy!"

I soon had a very original illustration of the truth of the last remark.

Both uncle and aunt had much family pride and were lovers of historic lore, and of everything that savored of antiquity. Eben knew the old colonial history of Plymouth thoroughly, and the family histories of most of the early settlers on the Cape, at Plymouth and on the shores of Massachusetts Bay.

One rainy afternoon, when I could neither walk, ride, nor sail, Uncle said to me:

"Do you draw?"

"I have taken lessons in drawing."

"I notice you have some large sheets of white paper, what do you call it?"

"Bristol board."

"Would you be willing to draw for me a family tree?"

"I will do as well as I can," and I at once went

to my room for paper and pencils, and on returning, asked how I should begin.

"Draw the roots, first."

"What ought he to write at the roots of the tree?" he said, turning to Aunt Desire.

"*My* family began with the Toogoods, of Cornwall. Zephaniah Toogood was a soldier in Cromwell's army. He was killed at the battle of Marston Moor."

Aunt Desire's cap-border seemed to rise after giving me this bit of family history, and she walked to and fro in a very sweet frame of mind.

"I can trace the Endicotts *further* back than that," said Uncle Eben, innocently. "The English revolution is of a comparative recent date."

Aunt Desire started. Her pride was touched. She moved her chair away from us and sat in silence, an unusual mood for her.

Uncle brought out of an old mahogany desk, some curious books and carefully-kept papers, and we spent several hours together carefully constructing a family tree. It was a very interesting occupation, although Aunt Desire's silence made me feel rather uncomfortable.

"Have you got through?" asked Aunt Desire, meekly.

"Yes," said uncle.

"Isn't it noble?" asked I. "I should think any family would be proud of a tree like that."

"That tree is all full of Endicotts, aint it?" asked Aunt Desire.

"Endicotts and their wives; a regular Endicott *pair* tree."

"How fur back does it go?"

"To the Plantagenets."

"Now, Jeff, I want you to draw *me* a family tree."

"A Toogood tree?" asked uncle. Aunt Desire did not answer.

"Certainly," said I. "Here is a full sheet of paper. How shall I begin?"

"I should begin away back to beginnin'," said Aunt Desire. "You might draw a little bioplasm and a little protoplasm, that Eben tells about, for the roots, and then write on one root 'Adam' and on another 'Eve.'"

"Next?"

"Cain and Abel," said Aunt Desire. "No, Cain didn't belong to our family. I should put merry 'The Jews.'"

"Well."

"King Solomon. He didn't do quite right in

all things, but I suppose I will have to own him."

"Next, put Alfred the Great," she added.

"And," said Aunt Desire, in a loud whisper, "leave out the Endicotts, when you get to them. I've heard that old Governor Endicott hung witches. I wouldn't want any such folks as those on *my* family tree, would you?"

Uncle Eben looked drolly at Aunt and me.

"I'll go and get tea now," said Aunt Desire." She went out with the air of one who was mistress of the situation, and that was the last I ever heard of the family tree.

But if Aunt was sometimes sharp to Uncle she was nevertheless true. He never had a sorrow or a pain that she did not suffer too. She anticipated his every want, and generally, except in one thing, did everything in her power to make his life happy.

This one exception is the point of my homely story, and I will clearly explain it here. Aunt was an ambitious woman. She was disappointed that Uncle was not a more ambitious man. She wished him to struggle for wealth and political honors. For years she had daily reminded him what he *might* have been.

When father's business was so successful that he purchased a stone-front house in a fashionable street in Boston, and furnished it with a good degree of elegance, Aunt Desire declared an open war of words against Uncle's contentment. Envy and jealousy led her often to say bitter things. Uncle kept an even temper, and I once overheard him say : —

"You have not seen the end of brother's affairs yet ; ambition and an expensive family are consuming him. I would not exchange places with him for his wealth. What you need, Desire, is a contented spirit and a thankful heart. This world is not our long home, Desire."

The overheard remark about father and his affairs troubled me. It left in my mind a presentiment of evil, that returned again and again like a shadow in my thoughtful hours. I loved Uncle and respected his opinions. I am sure he loved me, and he did what father seldom seemed to have time to do, made me his friend and expressed his affection for me.

He had never showed this spirit more than during this last visit. His own sons were well settled in the West. I could see that he was lonely at heart, and I was happy in his affectionate confidences. The more I associated with him the more father's condition and affairs troubled me; his life seemed to be a struggle for things that gave him no happiness, that left him no time for social or domestic affections, or independent thought, and that sooner or later would turn into dust. The question came again and again into my mind, — which will time prove the wiser and the better life, father's or Uncle Eben's?

# CHAPTER III.

MRS. DESIRE ENDICOTT DECIDES TO COME UP FROM THE CAPE.

"Now do hear that gal talk, Eben Endicott! And they always told that Boston wimmen was proud, too! Just as sure as you live, and as sartin as my name is Desire, I'm going to accept that there invitation. I've been wantin' to make a pilgrimage to Boston all my life.

"In the fust place, I want to go to the Monday Lectureship. There are a few things in heaven and on earth that I don't quite understand, and Parson White don't explain um at all to my satisfaction. Why, he don't even know who Melchizedek was! I asked him once in the Bible Class what made the grass green and the sky blue, and he couldn't tell; and then I made the simple inquiry as to whether there would be such a thing as sound if there was no one to hear it, and he couldn't answer that; and I don't think he could explain how it is a man raises his hand to his head.  What some people don't know in this world is amazin'.  But I shall have a chance to find out all about these unknowable things when I come up from the Cape, Carrie.

"Then, too, I want to hear some music before I die.  If I have one desire more than another, after havin' all the great mysteries of the past and future made clear to me, it is to hear the great organ.  They say some of the pipes are bigger 'n one's body, and that it takes a steam-engine to make it go.  Bless your soul! just think o' that, Ebenezer Endicott!  Wot you laughin' about, Carrie?  Aint it so?

"The fact is I'm musical myself, naturally.  You wouldn't think so, now would ye, but I used to sing in the choir.  I never told you what a dreadful mortification I experienced the fust time I sung in church, did I?  No, well, I will some day.  It is a sort of curious story, not of much account; do to tell some day after a clam-bake in the orchard.

"*First* was theology, *next* music.

"Well, I want to consult some o' those great physicians.  I've had some chronic troubles goin' on nigh upon twenty year.  I've been to all the physicians in Barnstable County, but they haven't done me any good. Why, would you believe it, they are so ignorant that each contradicts the other, and I don't get any satisfaction at all. There aint any two doctors on the Cape that has told me that the same thing ailed me, or that prescribed the same remedy, and I have used roots and yarbs until I am tired.

"Did ye ever read the doctors' advertisements in the Boston papers, Eben? Wonder o' wonders, what cures they do perform! Make ye all over scientifically, chipper as a milkmaid, and stout as a race-horse. I want advice in some place where the doctors are at least well enough educated to tell you the same thing, and recommend the same remedy.

"There is a little matter of law, too, that I want to know about, but that aint for your ears, Eben.

"Then, too, I want to see Richard Follett and his new wife. Dick has got rich, they say. He had a very hard time of it down here on the Cape. But it was in him to be somebody, and when that kind of a spirit is in a boy nothin' can stand against it. Ye can't make an eagle run round a barnyard like a hen, as Mr. Beecher says. But they do say that Dick is killin' himself with work, and is merely heapin' up money for an easy-going family to spend after he's dead and gone.

"I have also a bag full of poetry that I want to sell for Flora Pink, Jerry Pink's daughter. The Pinks are awful poor, and Flora is kind o' sickly and needs the money. The editors of those rich papers would be mighty small not to buy that poetry when I tell um all the circumstances under which it was written. Some of it was writ over the dye-tub, when that there gal was waitin' for the dye to set; and some of it was written at midnight. What do you think of that? Five of the pieces are on "Spring," and four on "Autumn." The last are very melancholy ones. Flora's put into my keeping poetry enough to supply all the editors of the city for a spell. Now, does poetry command a good fair price, Carrie?

"Well, I've been intending to go up from the Cape for forty years, and now, Eben, I've been invited, and by Carrie Endicott, too, whose father lives on the Back Bay, and keeps his carriage. And I'm goin', sure, and next fall, too. The Bible says, With all thy gettin's get wisdom. And Boston, as everybody knows, is the fountain-head of wisdom and learnin', from which all the streams of intelligence flow. A great many of the people know so much they go crazy, they say. I don't know how that may be; but Carrie, Carrie Endicott! you needn't laugh! You may depend upon it that next winter I'm comin' up from the Cape.

"Think of it, Eben Endicott! I never have been out of sight of the smoke of the chimbly all my days. Never had nothin' nor went anywhere. You've always been just contented with a few thousand dollars' worth of property and a lot of old books; and I've just done your cookin' and mendin', and gone neighborin' and to the camp-meetin's."

"*Only the light kind of people travel.*"

"Who says that, Eben? Emerson? I thought so. Solomon never said a thing like that."

"*St. Paul?*"

"What did he say? Yes, what *did* he say? That I must n't come up from the Cape?"

"*Therewith to be content.*"

"That's what he said, did he, Eben? Well, I don't care what he said. My mind's made up, Eben, and I'm just goin'. Now, there!

"There, he's gone out at last, Carrie. Think of what a man Eben might have been if he'd been ambitious like me, and had improved his opportunities. But you know what husband is, you know; he's a clever man, a very clever man, and a good provider and aforehanded, and he brought up his children well. Don't say nothin'; now that he's gone I will tell you that other reason why I want to come up from the Cape. That legal matter. He don't approve of what I did, husband didn't. You know what Eben is; he's a good man enough as men go, but no force like me. Don't ye never say nothin', I should feel dreadful bad if anything were to happen to Eben; he's always been a good provider, as I said, and always treated me well. I never asked him for anything in my life that he didn't go right off and get for me.

"It's a dead secret — what I'm about to tell ye. Don't mention it for the world. I've been *investin'*. Well, I ought to have had my dividends, five per cent *a month*, a year or two ago, but they don't come; they will be all the larger when they do come, but there is a sort of mysteriousness about the thing that I want to have cleared up. *That's* one of the reasons why I wish to come up from the Cape.

"It's a curious story, and I must tell you all about it. You may have heard me speak of Rev. Dr. Gamm. They used to call him the lighthouse preacher, he knew so much about everything. He certainly was very gifted in his tongue; it would go like a windmill on a March afternoon. He was a very social man, the doctor was. Husband used to say that he had the talent of veri similitude, whatever that might be.

"Well, the doctor was very unfortunate. He had a disease of the throat. It came upon him right in the prime of life, and compelled him to hide his light under a bushel, or, to speak more figuratively, the lighthouse went under a cloud. So he became an insurance agent. The company is all busted up now, but it paid him a great salary while it lasted, $3000 a year. His name appeared as treasurer on the advertisements of the company, although he told me that he really had nothing to do except to (write up) the company for the newspapers, and sign his name to such papers as the company sent to him, and to make out the reports.

"He grew very fat; his throat trouble was reduced to nothing but a 'hem,' and as his work was very light, he and his family used to board in different places, at fine hotels. He said that he looked upon the insurance business as the Lord's work, since it provided for the widow and the orphan, and so he left off preachin' altogether for a spell.

"Three summers ago he came down to Sandwich to look for a boardin' place for himself and family. He said that he would rather spend the summer at Sandwich than on the Vineyard, because he could go to the city or to the Vineyard from here any day as he liked. He thought he would like to board in a farm house for a change. I took him.

"One day as the Doctor and his family, husband and I, were settin' under the apple trees — I well remember the afternoon, for a shower was comin' up, and shadows of clouds were darkenin' the bay — the Doctor related to us a very interestin' story about a discovery that had been made by some of the Methodist brethren in New York. It made a very strong impression on my mind, but husband only said solemnly : —

"Dr. Gamm, people don't get something for nothing honestly." Sort of Emersonian talk, you see. "The Methodists are a clean people," says husband, says he. "They have had a clean record for one hundred years, and I am sorry that they should so far forget their primitive principles."

"Dr. Gamm sort o' collapsed. But his story set me all of a curiosity. It was something like this :

## TREASURE MOUNTAIN.

"There was a gentleman of enormous wealth in California, who was very ambitious to benefit the human race by doin' good — he had been well brought up and had not forgotten his early education. You know what Solomon says. Among this man's great possessions was Treasure Mountain, full of silver, and this mountain of silver he offered to the good Methodist brethren in New York to establish a university in the South for the education of young men for the ministry. A regular George Peabody, you see.

"Well, a company had been formed for the removal of Silver Mountain, with a capital of $10,000,000; but $50,000 was needed to put this mine, which reached from the earth to the heavens above, in workin' order, and this benevolent gentleman was willin' that certain Methodist', of good standin' and deservin' everyway, should subscribe to that amount, towards the operation of the mine, and he promised that the company would pay 5 per cent. a month on such investments.

"Five per cent. a month! That took me, I had five hundred dollars that I had been savin', and I took this out of the Saving Bank and let the Doctor have it to invest in Treasure Mountain for the benefit of the University; also for my own benefit. Husband didn't approve of what I did — but you know what husband is, you know; don't you ever say nothin', will ye?

"Well, 'tis mighty curious. I havn't received no dividends, nor heard anything of my $500 since. I hear that Dr. Gamm has an office in Boston, and I shall go to see him when I come up from the Cape.

"I read a paragraph in one of the papers a few weeks ago that don't sound quite right. I cut it out. Here it is:—

"The Methodist brethren who took stock in the T. M. Mine are now firm believers in the doctrine of original sin and total depravity. All new stock schemes are held in great disfavor at the Methodist headquarters. No promoter of a new mining enterprise could obtain a hearing among the dominies now, even if he should present a prospectus setting forth three-foot veins of silver covered with two-foot veins of gold, and edged with all the precious stones spoken of in the Book of Revelations."

"It makes me feel uneasy. I didn't like to show it to husband; you know what husband is, you know, a nice man and a good provider, and all that, but — well you won't never say anything, will ye, Carrie?"

# CHAPTER IV.

### EBEN FAVORS DESIRE'S PLANS AND ENTERTAINS CARRIE WITH HIS YOUTHFUL RECOLLECTIONS OF MRS. GREEN.

It was a mid-summer day. The old house was shaded by a cool corner of the old orchard. The doors and windows were open and we sat looking out upon the long meadows of Pocasset and the pleasant waters of Buzzard's Bay.

There was the same expression on the meadows and the sea. In every breeze that passed, the green meadows whitened with daisies, and green waters with foam. There was a clear atmosphere, full of sunshine over the sea; and the white wings of the gulls dipped listlessly through it on their zigzag way. Here and there hung a sail, like a broken wing, or a latine canvas of old.

The ospreys wheeled overhead and screamed. In the orchard an oriole flamed around its nest. In the old road now and then jogged a dilapidated vehicle, scattering the sand.

It was like a land of dreams. The world seemed to have gone off on a pic-nic, and to have left us alone, and in our faces was a contented look, as though we were glad to be left behind.

"Well, Desire, I am perfectly willing you should accept Carrie's invitation, but I want you to remember that wherever you may go you will find no more happiness, no more beauty, no more faith, hope and love, no more wealth, and no more worth than what you carry with you."

Desire pushed her spectacles up her nose, and put her hand half over her mouth and whispered obliquely to Carrie:

"Emerson. He just gets Emerson to think for him, husband does. *I* think for myself."

"A person need never go abroad for health," continued Uncle, "the conditions of good health are not outside of us but within us. And a person need never go wandering over the world to find the Lord; He's just as near to Buzzard's Bay as anywhere else."

"There, Eben, you've said enough, I never did yet get out of sight of the smoke of the chimbly."

"I ain't going to make any objections, Desire, to your going up to Boston from the Cape. I only hope you'll bring back with you as much happiness as you carry away.

"I'm contented to live and die right here in the old house where I was born. I've my Bible (and that is as good as the Lectureship) and Shakespeare, and all the best histories and poets, and when I want a little worldly wisdom I turn to Emerson, though Job said about all that Emerson has said, over again, thousands of years ago.

"And I am perfectly happy, I have no wish to go even to the fair, or the circus, or the theatre, or opera, or anywhere, but just to church on Sunday's, and the Friday evening meetings, town meetings and the yearly camp meeting. I make clambakes in the orchard for other people's enjoyment and not for my own. I like to see other people have a good time, and I am always willing to put my own feelings aside if it will help to make anybody happier.

"The greatest happiness we can have in this world comes from forgetting ourselves and in making others happy. He who denies himself the most receives the most from the Lord.

"Running after amusement always looked to me a very selfish thing. Pleasure flies from those who seek it, and comes unsought to those who do not think about it. A man should find the highest pleasures of life in his purpose and occupations.

Now, I am not hinting at you, Desire, I just want you to go wherever you wish to, and take all the comfort that you possibly can. I always gave free permission to my boys to go to any right place whenever they asked me.

"And the consequence was that they didn't care to go anywhere, but just stayed at home like their father, and read books and books. Then they went out West and became farmers, and *your* brother, Carrie, went to Paris. What do you think of that, even to Paris, where all those polite French people are that we read about in the geography."

"Did you never go to places of amusement, uncle?" I asked.

"Only a few times; that was when I was a boy. I don't object to such things when they are properly conducted, only they are not to my taste. The last theatrical performance I attended was some fifty years ago. I was one of the actors myself."

I asked for the story.

Uncle was a pleasant story-teller, when the subject was associated with his early life. He liked to relate historic stories, and humorous incidents of his boyhood and school days. The latter always pleased me, and I sometimes noted them down in my journal. So I will first introduce Uncle as a story teller, in his account of

### OUR ENTERTAINMENTS.

It was when I was at the Academy. One of the boys, named Brown, who was a great lover of Shakespeare, went to Boston and became stage-struck. When he came back he gave some performances in his room for the benefit of the class, and at last he suggested to us boys that it would be a capital plan, to get up, as he said, "some entertainments."

"We could begin with a concert, and, after some study, we could have amateur theatricals. We could at least give Othello strangling Desdemona. *That* would produce a thrilling effect, and would be something new in the Academy."

The idea of strangling Desdemona seemed to us very novel and picturesque and we favored it.

There was quite a number in our school who enjoyed a local reputation for their declamatory abilities. We had one comic genius, and a singer or two, and with this force we hoped to achieve success. The girls of our acquaintance all promised to come, if we bought tickets for them, and pronounced the idea "splendid!"

The only difficulty was in finding a suitable place in which to give our performance. The town-hall was out of the question, the vestries of the churches equally so, the school an impossibility, and no private house would answer provided we could secure one.

The only available place seemed to be a spacious hay-loft over Frank Green's barn. But, unfortunately, it would be about as well to ask Frank's mother for the use of her snapping black eyes as for her hay-loft.

Mrs. Green was one of those loud, demonstrative, hard-working women, who go stormfully through life, swift, strong and energetic, like a steam-engine, equally as noisy, and almost as dangerous if you stood in her way.

She was the terror of all the children, although really she was a kind-hearted woman in her own way. She was always ready to do a good turn and help a neighbor in distress, but she couldn't endure boys idling about her premises. She was sure they were trying to steal eggs, or fruit, or something or other belonging to her; and so she used to sally forth on them with her eyes aflame, clutching in her red right hand a most formidable cowhide.

I myself had two memorable encounters with the good lady. I once had to take a letter to a gentleman whose estate · adjoined hers; and, instead of going around and reaching it by the regular road, I leaped her wall and took a short cut across lots.

Just as I got about half way, what should I behold but Mrs. Green, cowhide in hand, accompanied by two dogs, bearing down on me! To run would be utter madness, because I should be certain to have the canine fangs buried in my flesh long before I reached the opposite wall. Strategy alone could help me in this awful emergency. Politeness and very humble bearing on my part might mollify my pursuer, and these mild weapons I resolved to use, encouraged by the recollection that discretion is the better part of valor.

My plan of defence was instantly conceived.

I stood still, and began looking about me as if bewildered.

Down swept the enemy upon me. Before she said a word — in fact, she didn't mean to speak much, except with the cowhide — I very politely asked her if she could inform me the nearest way to Mr. Anderson's. Her eyes flamed at me awhile, then, swallowing a lump in her throat, she pointed with her weapon the nearest way over the wall.  I thanked her with a bow and retreated without a glance behind, and felt extremely thankful when the stone wall was between us.

The other encounter forms the subject of this story.

Frank Green — a nice, quiet lad, like his late father — ascertained that his mother intended to go into the city soon, "for all day;" at which time we might have the hay-loft for our entertainment.

"First-rate!" we shouted.

"Then we'll have your hay-loft, Frank. We'll have plenty of time to get ready!" cried Brown.

"Plenty!" we shouted.

"Tip-top!" ejaculated Brown.  "And see, Frank, you can poke round up there, you know, in the meantime, and put things to rights — get the hay tucked away and cleaned up a bit, you know.  I s'pose it wouldn't do for one of *us* to go and help you?"

"'Twouldn't be well for mother to catch you, that's all!" said Frank, ominously.

"No!  Well, all right!  You'll do all that's wanted, Frank, in a quiet way, so as not to excite suspicion," said Brown. "And now, boys, you get your parts committed, and we'll have a rehearsal as soon as possible—next Saturday afternoon, perhaps, down back of old Smith's barn."

Brown, as I have suggested, was a forward, ambitious lad, and he took the whole management of the affair upon himself, although the suggestion was mine, in point of fact. Still I was, I confess, more apt at suggesting schemes than in carrying them into execution, and so very willingly conceded the work to my more energetic friend..

At length the memorable day arrived. It was as lovely a summer day as one could wish, just like this. A brightness over everything, and our hopes were high with the pleasure we were about to enjoy and afford our friends,—especially our girl-friends, who would, no doubt, be charmed with the performance.

Mrs. Green left for the city early in the day, and was not to be home before late in the afternoon. Nearly all the school would be our audience. Everything looked in a fair way for a brilliant success.

At half-past two, the hour appointed, we began climbing the rickety ladder that led up to the hay-loft. This, of itself, made no little sport, but created some delay on account of the timidity of the girls.

In the course of time, all were seated on such seats as could be improvised for the occasion. There were over twenty of us, all told, speakers and audience. One of the boys led off with a song, in such a harsh voice that we were really glad when he broke down in the third verse and retired amid the applause of the audience.

Brown, the ambitious Brown, was dressed in a stunning manner, and had no fewer than three pieces on the programme. His turn came next. He stepped to the platform, or, rather, what we called such, made a profound bow, and just as he uttered the words, "Ladies and Gentlemen," a voice from below shouting, "WHO'S UP THERE?" made my hair stand on end.

There was a dead silence.

"Ladies and gentlemen," continued Brown," "I arise to do you the honor of giving you a selection from Shakespeare. It is from 'Othello,' and I think you never saw anything like the performance that I am now about to perform." [He was right.) "I've been to Boston and have seen it done, and it brought tears to the aujunce's eyes.

"Othello, you know, was jealous of Desdemona, his wife. One day he came home and found her asleep, and determined to smother her with a bolster. This I shall now proceed to do."

The excitement was intense. Brown kicked together some loose hay, and threw his thin coat over it with the amazing declaration:

"*That* is Desdemona!"

He then took a large towel he had brought, and held it up:

"*That* is the bolster."

Brown struck an attitude, and in a deep voice approached the supposed Desdemona on her couch.

"*I will kill thee!*"

"*I say*," said a strange, hesitating voice, not at all in the programme.

There was a short silence, then Brown proceeded.

"I must weep." [And he did.] "*But they are cruel tears. She wakes!*"

Then, in a squeaking voice, supposed to represent the waking Desdemona, he said:

"*Who's there? Othello?*"

"*I say, who's there?*"

This latter question was hardly an echo. The voice seemed to come up from below.

But Brown was full of his subject now, and proceeded in a high voice:

"*Thou art to die!*"

He then added in a changed voice, supposed to be Desdemona's:

"*The Lord have mercy on me!*"

Brown next bent over the bundle of hay and proceeded to smother the helpless wife. A strange, convulsive sound, as of one in mortal agony, seemed to issue from the old coat and hay. It was a thrilling moment.

"*I say, who's up there on the mow? I want to know right off, now!*"

It was Mrs. Green!

She wasn't on the programme.

"I say, *who's there?*" said the voice in such a resolute tone as caused us all to start.

There was profound silence.

"I hear some one up in that loft; *come down*, I say, at once!"

"*I'm* up here, mother," said Frank, with pale lips.

"Yes, and who else? It wasn't your voice I heard. *Is there any one else there?* Tell me before I come up with the cowhide!"

THE BARN THEATRICALS.

"Oh, then and there was hurrying to and fro,
And gathering tears, and tremblings of distress."

Yes, it was a fearful moment, and to this day, after the lapse of thirty years, I remember my own sensations. Frank was the first to descend; and the sound of the cowhide on his jacket was no means encouraging.

One after another we dropped to the floor, where the amiable old lady was applying the cowhide in a most vigorous style, uttering all kinds of threats and exclamations with equal force and perseverance.

At last the skirts began to make their appearance.

"What! — Girls!"

This apparition completely bewildered her. Boys were bad enough, but girls fairly paralyzed her arm for a moment, so that the cowhide dropped at her side.

But Mrs. Green was equal to the occasion and faithfully did her duty.

"Jane, is *that* you?"

Whack! Whack!

"Liddy, is *that* you?"

Whack! Whack!

"Thankful, is *that* you?"

Whack! Whack!

And in this uniform manner each girl as she descended the ladder of the improvised theatre was met, and given an inspiration which accelerated her movements in the nearest direction towards home.

I was not forgotton in the general discipline. I had all the entertainments I cared to receive that afternoon, and I have not been to any place of amusement since. I did not even go to see the "Pinafore.'

## CHAPTER V.

#### THE OLD ORCHARD AND BURYING-GROUND.

The charm of a small farm on the New England Coast is usually its orchard. An old apple orchard in Barnstable County and the Bay towns has beauties that no city forrester could produce in his imitations of Italian gardens. From the time that the blue-birds arrive and the red-headed woodpeckers first show their mottled wings on the dead boughs until the last pippin falls there is pleasure to be taken in the orchard. When the orioles and thrushes come, and the arms of the trees are filled with blooms; when the air is full of the songs of robins and the passing breezes with delicious, almost suffocating odors; when the listless May days return with the hum of bees, and the slightest stir in the air sends down showers of broken blossoms in creamy flakes upon the emerald turf; in dewy June mornings and celestial mid-summer days; in early autumn and late autumn when the falling of the fruit follows the falling of the blossoms and when at last the dropping of the russet leaves ends all, it seems as though something Paradisic remained in the mossy old trees, and one is reminded that the same Hand that fashioned the immortal gardens gave the world such scenes as these whose beauties the resurrective power of the spring-time eternally renews.

The orchard at uncle's was indeed a noble one; it had grown into mossy colonnades in the salt air of more than fifty years. The dead limbs were full of wood-pecker's holes, the certain evidences of age. Into the abandoned nests of the wood-peckers of other years, the wrens and blue-birds swarmed.

Wherever else the air was close and sultry, the orchard was always cool. The poultry loved the orchard, and the peacock announced the coming storm from its bars. The children of two generations had played there, looking into the birds' nests in the spring, and fighting mimic battles, like Francis I. with the oranges, in the fall.

At one end of the orchard was the ruin of a cider mill. Here in anti-temperance days the waste apples were ground. It was a ruin worthy of an artist, and one too that was suggestive of progress and moral reform.

The cider-makers were a vanished race, but one old custom associated with the apple harvest, Eben steadily maintained, it was the Apple Parin'.

Eben's "Apple Parin's" were famous. The neighbors came to them from far and near. That two patent paring-machines would have done as much work as all the invited guests, did not matter. It was an old-time custom, and one against which nothing evil could be said.

Eben prided himself on his story telling as much as a star lecturer on his new fall lecture. These "apple parins" gave him an opportunity to rehearse the old stories of Plymouth, the Cape and the Islands.

There was not a legend of colonial times with which he was not familiar, whether of the Cape towns or the harbor towns of Massachusetts Bay. The old Indian history from the time that Verassano, the Florentine, first saw the ancestors of Massasoit, was better known to him than to any writer on the subject I have ever read. He was a careful reader of Drake, and almost always was able to add to this historian's narrations some legend or story of equal interest, if of less value.

Eben was also a poet, and he sometimes read a

poem at the "Parin' Bee." Music of flute and fiddle, songs, story telling, and an occasional poem, made these simple gatherings delightful occasions. Many love-makings had begun here, and several proposals of marriage had been bashfully made by rustic lovers in the full moonlight, as they returned from Uncle Eben's.

The great attraction of these merry-makings to older persons was the supper. Aunt Desire was a natural cook, and she put her pride and reputation into every dish and loaf of bread prepared for the "bee." Her brown bread was heavy with plums, and even her baked sweet apples were dusted with sugar. Her roast meats had all the same shade of brown, and her "slumps," as she called the enormous pot apple pies, were so crusted with "sweetenin'" that they were as toothsome as candy.

The orchard wall was filled with old green mosses. Robins made their nests among them. On the wall near the porch was a row of house leeks, and under it a long line of currant bushes.

Beyond the orchard and the ruined cider mill was the old neighborhood burying ground. The way to it wound around the orchard and was shaded by cherry trees. From the burying ground we had an extended view of Buzzard's Bay and the Islands.

The grave yard was nearly two centuries old. The pioneers, of the days of Queen Anne and the Georges rested here under dark slate stones, with dreadful effigies. Here slept three generations of the Endicotts, and here the old preachers of Calvinistic faith and Cromwellian courage.

I used to go to the place with Uncle on Sunday afternoons, and sit under the one solitary tree that cast a shadow in this open town of the dead. Uncle seemed to love the spot.

I said to him one day while we were there.
"Life seems to me all a mystery — I wish I knew what is farther on."

He laid his hand in mine, thoughtfully:

"If you would know what is farther on, you must go farther on," he said, "Life is a mystery. We have come out of the past, and what our ancestors were largely determines what we are now. We know more in childhood than in infancy: more in manhood than boyhood, and the horizon of life grows broader with age. Evolutions of the past have produced us, and landed us on life's mysterious shores. Other evolutions await us. We shall lose this material covering, and the soul will go forth into the infancy of a new life to progress and expand — infinity is before us.

> "The stars are but the shining dust
> Of my divine abode,
> The pavements of those heavenly courts
> Where I shall dwell with God."

"I wish to believe as you do," said I, "but I can arrive to no conclusion; the great teachers of religion tell me such different and contradictory things. I look around me and what do I see? The Romish church condemns the Protestant church as heretical, and the Protestant world holds Rome to be Anti-Christ; each sends the other to doom and loss. The Greek church condemns both. Even the Protestant church is full of sects which teach different ways of salvation, and each condemns the ways of the others. The creeds of fifty churches in Boston contradict each other. Only one can be right — good men teach them all — what am I to believe? Science explains nothing; whence we came, why we are here, or whither we are going.

"I wish to know the truth and to practice it. Your life and example make me wish to think rightly and do rightly. Every young man at times thinks as I do now, and is perplexed as I am perplexed."

"My boy," said uncle, "the truths that Christ taught to the woman at the well of Samaria will never contradict human experience, or change. The old beliefs are going and I do not regret their loss, but these truths will eternally stand; every good that one does will be rewarded, and every evil punished, and the pure spiritual life that the gospel teaches is the best condition of the soul. We have an evil nature. We can change it into a good nature, and over that change the gates of heaven open and glow. Christ made that change possible, and preached it as the need of the world. I believe in churches — they are God's agents — but no church can unchurch any man who has within him this spiritual life. These truths will never change."

His remarks impressed me, and for the first time in my life, I read that night the book of John.

There was one stone in the windy old grave-yard that rose above the others. Uncle told me that he erected it at his own expense out of regard to a most unselfish and true man. Under the name "Bonny" were these curious lines :—

> "No foot of land do I possess,
> No cottage in the wilderness,
> A poor wayfaring man."

I one Sunday asked uncle the purport of this strange inscription, and he related to me this beautiful account of one of the old Cape ministers:—

### A HILLSIDE STORY.

"It is not so much what we do for ourselves as what we do for others that brings us love and influence.

John Wesley was a self-forgetful man. He died poor, and his refusal of money for more than needful purposes was one of the sources of his marvellous influence over men. At the age of forty, when the storm of persecution had spent its force, and the fruits of his labor began to appear, he wrote the once famous hymn beginning, "How happy is the pilgrim's lot." In this hymn he gave an incident of his own experience as follows:—

> "No foot of land do I possess,
> No cottage in the wilderness,
> A poor wayfaring man:
> I lodge awhile in tents below,
> Or gladly wander to and fro,
> Till I my Canaan gain,"

This was literally true. When he and John Nelson began to preach among the rough seafaring population of Cornwall, no one would give them a meal's victuals. "We used to preach, and then dine off the blackberry bushes," he said. Before he died he was accustomed to preach from an hillside pulpit to congregations of thirty thousand people in Cornwall, and both in the nobleman's castle and the peasant's hut he would have been a welcome and an honored guest.

The old travelling preachers in New England, and the then West in the times of Jesse Lee, were greatly influenced by the reformer's example in respect to their worldly affairs. They were often treated with disrespect, but their hardships seemed to heighten their spiritual life, and to renew their confidence in their Master's assurance of final triumph here and future reward hereafter.

One of these "circuit riders," or "saddle-bag preachers," as they were sometimes called, was Father Bonny. He rode thousands of miles in a year, and he almost always prefaced a sermon by singing the hymn I have quoted, or another beginning,—

"Come on, my partners in distress,
 My comrades in the wilderness,
 Who still your bodies feel."

A rich village esquire, who was a man of generous impulses, but wholly indifferent to religion, often entertained Father Bonny on his annual visits to the town.

"The old man shall not have occasion to sing 'No foot of land do I possess' any more," he said one day to his wife. "To-morrow is Thanksgiving, and I am going to give him something at last to be thankful for. Now that we have moved into our new house, I think I will give him the deed of the old homestead and the ten-acre lot. We shall not miss the property. It belonged to my father. I want it kept as of old."

He fulfilled his intention, and the old circuit rider accepted the present with evident joy and gratitude.

A year passed. Again Thanksgiving came, and Father Bonny was expected to return to the town and preach. He arrived at last, a white-haired, trembling old man, and immediately went to the stately house of the esquire, who the year before, had made him the thanksgiving present.

Almost his first words were, "You must take it

back, Squire. It takes away my comfort when I sing *my* hymn."

"Take what back?" asked the astonished esquire.

"The house and lot, and then I can go to the school-house and preach and sing *my* hymn in peace."

"But I thought you'd be thankful for it," said the esquire.

"Squire, you will not understand me in this matter, I am sure. I wish you could. But you will believe me when I say that I have things to be thankful for of which you are ignorant. You cannot appreciate them, because you have not experienced their blessed effects upon the heart and life. Here is the deed. Take it."

The esquire took it hesitatingly, but in silence. As the deed left the old man's hand a holy calm came into his face. He leaned back in the chair, pressed his hands together and sang, in a trembling voice, —

> "How happy is the pilgrim's lot,
> How free from every anxious thought,
> From earthly hope or fear."

His face fairly beamed with happiness when he came to the line, "No foot of land do I possess."

"Squire," he said, "would you know why I am so happy? Listen to the next verse:

> "*There* is a house, my portion fair,
> My treasure and my heart are there,
> And my abiding home."

His voice faltered, but he presently added, —

> "The angels beckon me away,
> And Jesus bids me come."

"Squire, I am not feeling well. I am sick. I think my work is almost done."

So it was. The village esquire saw the truth. There were things to be thankful for that he knew not of. They were more than wealth. They were the marvellous spiritual perceptions, that are supernatural gifts, by which a man knows that God loves him and he loves God. It is not delusion. This love of his God and the consciousness of nearness to him had moulded the whole life of this self-denying man. They had made him a blessing to others, and had lighted the future with a brightness that made the grave a portal of delight. Such experiences are born of heaven and not of earth.

I had begun to take more serious views of life under uncle's influence. The good man noticed the change, and it seemed to give him great pleasure. As I have said, he sometimes wrote poems, homely rhymes, yet agreeable renderings of wholesome truths and helpful illustrations of right living. Soon after the talks I have given, I found on my table, one night, these lines. I put them in my note-book after reading, and I have since read them thoughtfully many times. They have helped me, plain as they are.

### TO JEFFERSON.

#### I.

When the false teachers rise, more subtile than wise,
    Who the faith of the good would destroy,
Who would rob you at last of the gold of the skies,
    And leave you but earthly alloy,
        Believe them not.
    Each evil you do will prove sorrow to you,
        And each virtuous action a joy;
    Be true to yourself and to others be true,
        And be true to your Maker, my boy.

#### II.

They may say the Designer came from the design,
    That evil was meant to enjoy,
That the striving for wealth and the babble of wine
    Of the soul are a fitting employ.
        Believe them not.
    For each evil you do will prove sorrow to you,
        And each virtuous action a joy;
    Be true to yourself and to others be true,
        And be true to your Maker, my boy.

### III.

The soul in dead matter received not its birth,
  Nor the thoughts that the senses employ;
And no long evolution has passed o'er the earth
  Without an Evolver, my boy.
      Believe them not.
  Each evil you do will prove sorrow to you,
    And each virtuous action a joy;
  Be true to yourself and to others be true,
    And true to your Maker, my boy.

### IV.

The soul is a growth in the good or the ill,
  Each virtue toward heaven ascends;
Each noble act strengthens the wing of the will,
  And evil to permanence tends.
      Believe them not.
  Each evil you do will prove sorrow to you,
    And each virtuous action a joy;
  Be true to yourself and to others be true,
    And true to your Maker, my boy.

### V.

Whate'er they may say, be sure the false way
  Will leave you at last but life's scars;
The lights and the flash of the gilded saloon
  Are not the pure rays of the stars.
      Believe them not.
  Each evil you do one day you will rue,
    When death shall life's prospects destroy;
  Then be true to yourself and to others be true,
    And true to your Maker, my boy.

### VI.

The guide of the soul is the old Bible still,
  And the teacher of spiritual joy,

And he only finds loss, let him go where he will,
Who turns from its counsels, my boy.
        Believe them not.
For each evil you do will prove sorrow to you,
   Whatever your hands may employ,
Then be true to yourself and to others be true,
   And true to the Master, my boy.
UNCLE EBEN.

# CHAPTER VI.

### AUNT EXPRESSES HER OPINION OF SISTER CARRIE'S BEAU.

"Jeff — Jefferson, sit down here, under the woodbine. I don't like to say it, but I can't help it; I don't like your sister Carrie's beau at all, that Rev. Mr. Glass. He hasn't any blood in him, no eyesight to speak of, and he talks through his nose.

"Then, too, I can't understand half that he says, can you? Yesterday he said to uncle as I was cookin', that 'everything was tendin' to the complete and possible pan.'

"'The complete and possible pan!' After all the trouble I had had on the Cape with the tin-peddlers, I was glad to know that an ample and possible pan was to be the outcome of everything at last, but as that kind of pan would be a rather meagre result of the 'evolutionary processes of creation,' as he called it, I concluded that some other kind of pan must be meant.

"There is one question that always puzzled me, I wonder if it ever troubled anyone else; it is why evil should be in the world at all? So I thought I would ask Rev. Mr. Glass.

"'Evil,' said he, 'is the remnant of our old animal nature — the old animal in us, so to speak, not yet wholly eliminated in the rise of man.'

"I clapped both hands to my cap-strings. 'Evil is the old animals left in us in the rise of man! You don't think, Mr Glass, that man was once an animal?'

"'Certainly, madam.'

"'And what shall we be next?'

"'Man is rising, madam,' said he, 'rising. The time will come when man will no longer talk, but will communicate thought by mental impressions; when he will no longer eat, but assimilate; when he will no longer wear clothing, but will be surrounded by a radiation, a halo; and there will come a time, madam, when it will no longer be fashionable to wear the body at all.'

"'That's so,' said I. 'It isn't fashionable to wear the body a great while, even now. How long do you think it will be before that time will come, Mr. Glass?'

"He said something about 'multifarious ages,'

and, law, I couldn't understand him, no more than I could a blackbird. If a man's got anything to say, why don't he say it, and not go all around Robin Hood's barn, that way?

"I am naturally fond of music. I can sing nearly all the tunes in Gospel Hymns No. 1, 2, and 3, and the singing of those hymns and tunes has made me a better woman.

"One day, as Mr. Glass stood leaning on the banister in a very 'staturesque' way, as Carrie calls it when he stands on one foot, with the toe of his other foot just touching the floor, one knee crooked like one's elbow, he said to me with a far off look in his face.

"'Who is your favorite composer?'

"'P. P. Bliss,' said I.

"'Bliss, Bliss'— he seemed thinking over the great names of the past, sort of wandering through the Middle Ages — 'Bliss, — how strange, I never heard of him.'

"'More than twelve million copies of his books have been sold,' said I. 'Sell like hot cakes in England, Scotland and Ireland too. Why, every child knows the *compositions* of P. P. Bliss.'

"'Extraordinary.' He drummed with his fingers absently on the banister. 'Mr. Bliss must be an

American composer, else I would have known of him.'

"'Yes, he is an American composer,' said I, 'and my opinion is that his hymns and tunes have done more to help the honest people of America to a better and happier life than any other man. I think that that man is the best writer, whether it be of books or music, who does the most good in the world : don't you, Mr. Glass?"

"'I see, Madam, you value art merely as an influence on character and as an educator of the spiritual sentiments. A provincial musician, like Tom Moore, would satisfy a taste like that. With *us*, the case is different. We value art for art alone. We do not value it for its influence on character at all. We do not value it either for the light and hope it may bring to common souls.'

"'Then what is the good of it?'

"'If you had had an artistic training the question would have been superfluous, madam. The principle is this — art is art. The great artist does not seek to apply it to vulgar uses. If you were to attend one of the concerts of the Thalia Club you would get my idea better. Classical art can only be understood by illustration. — P. P. Bliss : Bliss, an American composer; has had much influence among American people. Strange I never heard of him. The fact is I do not read American papers; occasionally look over the *National*, that is about the only American paper we Club House men ever read.'

"He continued to drum on the banister with the same far-away look in his eyes. I thought he must be in a sort of artistic rapture; spell-bound, so to speak, but after he had gone, I happened to glance up at the corner bracket to which his attention had been directed, and what do you think I saw there? The statue of Prayin' Samuel, that used to be there? No, Carrie had taken that down and put up a *looking-glass*.

"Now, a man like that can't have any good sense. What could he do to support a family? That's the kind of people they make institutions of — I mean asylums and such.

"I mean to have a square talk with Carrie, some day. I don't care if he was a Harvard divinity student. I want Carrie Endicott to remember that she has got Puritan blood in her veins, and when she marries, I hope it will be to a man, and not to a boy whose legs are too airy to hang his hat on. You don't like such people, now do you, Jefferson?"

# CHAPTER VII.

I RECEIVE A STRANGE LETTER FROM FATHER.

Riding, boating, wandering over the sandy hills, helping Uncle Eben! How pleasantly the summer days passed, and how like a home indeed seemed the old house where my ancestors had lived and died!

I had written to father for some money — a moderate amount — and in my letter I had spoken of my affectionate respect for Uncle Eben, and my interest in his opinions and the helps and comforts of his simple, democratic way of life.

Father had never been confidential with me. He seemed to be ambitious that I should be well educated and should go into good society — that was all. I never ran to his easy-chair to tell him my little affairs, to kiss him good night, or took arm-in-arm walks with him. Other boys did these things. I envied them.

I received an answer to my letter that at once made me happy yet apprehensive of some impending evil. It kindled a flame of real affection in my heart, yet left me ill at ease. With the sunlight came a cloud.

It read as follows:—

Hotel Wellesley,<br>July 20th.

My dear Son:—And I can truly say, *dear son*. I have not shown you much sympathy or affection, and I have expressed to you none; but something that you have done almost unconsciously has turned my thoughts constantly to you for the last three weeks, and has brought into my experience a strong sense of love for you. It is the only happiness I have.

It was this: you said to Carrie that you wished to spend the summer in such a way as to make me as little expense as possible. How different is this from the conduct of the rest of the family! It showed me that you saw that I was overworking, was troubled, and that you have at heart some real regard for me.

The small amount of money for which you now ask, and which I send, shows, also, that what you said was not mere sentiment. Your expressed regard for Brother Eben and his simple republican home, accords now with my own feelings. Jefferson, let me say to you what I have not said in my letters to any other member of my family, — I love you!

I wish to tell you privately that I am greatly troubled about my business affairs. At times my brain burns. I get up at night, for I cannot sleep much, and I walk, walk. It is very beautiful here, — the great pine groves, the winding Charles, the hills, the gardens, and the prospect of the college.  But your mother is not satisfied; she says it is too quiet for her, socially, and she has decided to spend the rest of the season in Newport. I shall return to my home in the city.  I have no heart to go to Newport, haunted as I am by business secrets that I can share with no one.

Your brother in Paris seems to me very thoughtless and extravagant.  He has just asked me for another draft of £250.  His letter is filled with descriptions of fashionable life, — all about the "swells" at Etretat, — and expresses no regard for me.  How heartless it seems beside of yours!

Jefferson, I have made some mistakes in life.  I engaged in speculation to meet the expenses of a very ambitious family.  My ventures were very successful for a time; they have not been so of late.  I hope it will end well.

I have not made friends of my family; the excitements and demands of business have left me no time. I have not had time to think and read books, or to cultivate a religious faith, like Eben.  I have not had time to care for my own health.  The consequence is that this world seems to me empty and selfish, and the future dark and hopeless.  My health is breaking at forty-two.  I cannot sleep, as I have told you; my brain is always awake.  I have no one but you to love me.  I sometimes wish I had followed the traditions of my family, and had lived as simple but true a life as your Uncle Eben's.

I think of the Cape constantly; of the old house, the orchard, the burying-ground.  If I were to die suddenly

I would wish to be buried there, where brother would care for my grave. I have a presentiment of coming misfortune. I can feel a shadow beginning to steal over the sun, though it has yet only touched it. If anything happens to me I wish you to go to live with Eben. He will speak charitably of me to you; he will understand. You are my own true son.

Remember me always, whatever may happen, as

            Your loving father,

                HENRY ENDICOTT.

I read this letter over twenty times. I did not show it to Carrie. I withheld it from Uncle for I knew that there were some things in it that would cause him pain. What was I to infer from it?

Many things, as my story will show. It had one immediate effect — it made me love my father more than any one in the world, and resolve to be true to him and his interests. It gave to my life two elements it needed, affection and a purpose.

CAPE CLAM-BAKE.

## CHAPTER VIII.

THE CLAM-BAKE, AND STORY-TELLING UNDER THE TREES.

The clam-bakes in Uncle Eben's orchard were famous in the towns of the Cape. Several church societies held their "annual" clam-bakes there; mid-summer "feasts of tabernacles;" gatherings of rustic simplicity, such as are known only on the Rhode Island and Massachusetts coast. A Western man, a Southerner, or a foreigner can have little conception of the social charm of these provincial merry-makings. Almost every church society on or near the Southern New England coast has its annual clam-bake.

In fact many of the churches in the country and small towns depend upon the profits of this out-of-door festival to make up the deficits in their "running expenses" and in the minister's small salary.

"How do you raise your minister's salary?" I once asked of a deacon who lived in one of the small coast towns.

"We pay him well; he's first-class, and an amazing smart preacher. I don't know how we would get along if it wern't for the clam-bake. Last year we had *two*."

The clam-bake is of Indian origin. How it became a kind of church festival we cannot tell. Its customs are peculiar to itself. The clam-bakes at the popular summer resorts have little in common with them.

When the "trustees" of some rustic church decide that they have a clam-bake, the members of the church and society feel that they are bound to give it their practical support.

A few days before the feast the men and boys of the church and society go "clamming" twice a day, at the low tides. Each has his hoe and basket, and the bivalves which they dig are placed in a common pile.

On the day before the great event, a party of men go fishing, giving their time and its results to the common cause.

While the men are thus preparing for the rustic feast, the women are as busy making brown-bread, white-bread, "stuffings," puddings and pies for the same purpose. These preparations are the topic of talk of the neighborhood.

The day arrives, almost always a fine one—usually in August "after haying." The sun comes up blazing over the sea, coloring the thin fogs as they roll away, and lighting up the half of each white sail that drifts along the watery horizon.

The air is cool and refreshing, after the last evening's heat. The birds sing in the old orchards; the dew quickly disappears, filling the air with the odor of new-mown hay in its drying.

At an early hour the "trustees" prepare on the ground in a grove or orchard a "bake-hole" of "live" stones, and put upon the stones a huge pile of cord-wood.

The wood is lighted; the smoke curls into the light air, a great flame arises and is fed by logs of seasoned wood for some two hours. The "live" stones are thus heated, and into this simple oven from ten to forty bushels of clams and a great quantity of fish, together with Irish potatoes and sweet potatoes and green corn are placed, and are baked under the direction of a "manager" who must be a man of experience, judgment and skill in such matters, or the "bake" may come out "raw" or underdone, and prove a failure.

The orchards or groves where these festivals are held are usually on hill-sides or on some part of the coast over-looking the sea. They are leafy and cool, with an over-tide of summer sunlight glimmering through the boughs.

The tables for the feast, of rude boards, are picturesquely spread under the arches of young apples or acorns. The ospreys wheel and scream in the air above, and the locusts sing in the tree-tops.

In the middle of the forenoon the gathering begins. Every vehicle from the houses for miles around comes loaded with the young, middle-aged and old; all in holiday dress or Sunday clothes. Aged people who do not meet oftener are sure to renew their old friendships at the clam-bake once a year, and relate to each other an annual chapter of their uneventful lives: their fluctuations of health, their rheumatisms, when they heard last "from brother Jeems's wife," and how the Cobb family "out west," are getting along.

The women bring contributions of new made butter, and dressings, pies and cake.

As soon as the bake-hole is "open," the feast is hurriedly served, while the clams and fish are "hot." The young people are in high spirits; it is a merry, chatty scene; simple and innocent. No poet has sung it; no painter attempted to paint it.

After the dinner 'remarks' are made by the pastor, and by 'invited guests' who are generally from the city and pay for their entertainment in contributions of cheap jokes and small talk. Songs are sung, and the rest of the day is devoted to recreations, swinging, croquet, boating, confidential talks, and more singing.

Aunt Desire was the soul of benevolence at these rural festivals. Her rooms were open to the old and young; she supplied from her own cupboards any articles for which provision had not been made, and usually attended to the cooking of the dressings, a matter that required especial care.

After the dinner was over the children would gather around her in some quiet place under the trees, and ask her for stories of old Colony times. These were not only interesting in themselves, but she usually added somewhat to their charm by giving cookies to all her appreciative hearers; and as aunt's cookies were unequalled she never lacked an audience.

One of the small societies of one of the Plymouth county towns had arranged with Uncle Eben for a clam-bake and picnic in the orchard. The church was poor, and Aunt Desire took an especial interest in this gathering for that reason. She invited the Rev. Mr. Glass to remain a few days longer than he had intended, so as to "enjoy the bake" and address the children. She remarked to me that she did not think that what my clerical friend would say would be of much interest or value, but that it "would be handy to have a Boston minister on the grounds, just for the name of it, you know."

Aunt made preparation for the gathering by baking "three stone jars full of cookies," as she expressed the result of her labors over the oven, one sultry August morning.

"And now, Carrie," she said to my sister, "I want you to think out a Boston story to tell to the children, a real pretty one, something that will do us credit."

Mr. Glass had never seen one of these shore dinners. He seemed to take much interest in it, and remarked to me, that this was "something extraordinary, really remarkable." He even helped bring wood for feeding the fire of the stone oven, until a snake chanced to run out of the wood pile, "a wiggling reptile, that might be poisonous," that caused him to make a sudden retreat, and look upon that part of the field of operations with a disturbed and hesitating countenance.

Aunt had her usual audience after dinner. More, not only the children gathered around her, and sung their songs, but many old people, who sung several camp-meeting hymns, and talked of the manners and customs of other days.

### A STARTLED CHURCH CHOIR.

"A story?" said Aunt Desire. "Well, there's nothin' disobleegin' about me. I am always ready to talk when any wants to hear me. Some of my friends do not always want to hear me: husband for instance. *Have some cookies?*

"Well, I think of one that will perhaps please the young people and old people too. It happened long ago, nigh upon fifty years.

"The old Orthodox society in the town where I lived when I was a girl, had much trouble about their singin'. The young folks wanted a choir, and the old folks didn't, and it made a sort of division. Those who favored singin' by the congregation quoted the passage 'Let all the people praise thee;' and those who wanted a choir answered with, 'Let all things be done decently and in order.' *Have a cookee?*

"At last the deacons consented to have a choir. Now I have a powerful voice, naturally, though I can't sing as I used to, and I'd been to the singin' school, and knew the notes. Miss Flinn agreed to sing alto, the schoolmaster, tenor, and Timothy Toogood, base, and I was chosen to be the soprano, which made me the head singer of all.

"We met to practice and we astonished ourselves by the music we made. I laid awake nights thinkin' how we would astonish other people on Sunday.

"And we did.

"We concluded to open the services by a voluntary, that is, a piece not in the old hymn-book, a sort of free offerin', as it were. It was a beautiful piece we selected; I remember it now. It was what I call poetry.

"Repeat it? Well, I will. *Have some cookies?*

"In the tempest of life, when the wave and the gale
Are around and above, if thy footing should fail,
If thine eye should grow dim, and thy caution depart
'Look aloft!' and be firm, and be fearless of heart.

"If the friend who embraced in prosperity's glow,
With a smile for each joy and a tear for each woe,
Should betray thee when sorrows like clouds are arrayed,
'Look aloft!' to the friendship which never shall fade.

"Should the visions which hope spreads in light to thine eye
Like the tints of the rainbow, but brighten to fly,
Then turn, and through tears of repentant regret,
'Look aloft!' to the Sun that is never to set.

"Should they who are dearest, the son of thy heart,
 The wife of thy bosom, in sorrow depart,
'Look aloft,' from the darkness and dust of the tomb,
 To that soil where affection is ever in bloom."

"There, I call that poetry, don't you? None of your 'Pull for the Shore' verses, although that piece is all well enough in its place, but genuine sentiment.

"It was a pleasant Sabbath and the church was crowded. I felt a kind of trepidation come over me as I looked from the gallery on the heads bobbin' below, and my heart was all in a flutter. Every stroke of the bell smote me like a knell of doom, and, as the people kept pilin' into the church and castin' sly looks towards the gallery, I wished a hundred times, like the poet, for a lodge in some vast wilderness. At length the bell ceased tolling, and the people were all ears. I got up nervously, my limbs trembling all over, and my mouth as dry as a chip. We formed a line, the bass viol banged and squeaked, and at last all was ready. I gasped once or twice, then I started off at the top of my voice, in a manner that was astonishing. I made the arches ring. I begun to feel as proud as a *prima donna*. A part of the piece was very high and afforded me an opportunity to display my strength of voice.

"Just as I was singin' the 'Look Aloft' in the second verse, who should come hobbling into the gallery but old Dame Rider, followed by her yellow dog. I hate dogs in general, and hated this one in particular, for he always seemed to owe me a grudge.

"A pitcher partly filled with water, stood on the floor not far from my feet. The dog trotted forward, casting an evil eye at me, and jammed his head into the pitcher. I sang 'Look aloft' as loud as ever I could, and then looked at the dog.

"He had put his head into the pitcher so far that he couldn't get it out, and was backing towards me with the pitcher on his head, bowing in a way that appeared very polite. The rest of the choir tittered, but the thought of what might happen if the dog should break the pitcher or slip it off, filled me with terror.

"'Look aloft,'" I screamed.

"I didn't look aloft myself, but straight at the dog, which was wiggling, howling and yelping close to my heels, and pushin' against me with the pitcher snugly fitted to his head and neck.

"I kicked him spitefully, then sung 'Look aloft' again, in a terrific manner, myself looking at the dog. He moved off a little and I ventured

LOOK ALOFT.

a glance at the congregation. They were indeed looking aloft, and at your humble servant most enquiringly.

"A happy thought struck me. I would let them know the cause of my agitation. So I sung 'Look aloft,' louder than ever. They all looked, and I added in a twinkling:

"'Get out, you dog.'

"I put out my foot and gave him a push, and what do you think that dog did? He backed right over the railing of the gallery, and tumbled, howling and yelping, into old Mrs. Toogood's pew below. Mrs. Toogood was looking aloft when the accident happened.

"Everybody was grinning in a most improper manner. I finished the piece, and we didn't sing any more that day. We started for home as soon as the benediction was pronounced, and didn't dare to look to the right hand nor to the left, nor even aloft.

"But next Sunday we opened with 'Haddam,' and we had 'um for sure. Everybody was delighted, and our choir went on without any quarrel for more than three months. Was there ever heard anything equal to that? *Have some more cookies, all of you, now do. Don't be sparin', plenty more where these came from.*

Now, children, my niece here, Carrie Endicott, will tell you a Boston story. Sit down, Mr. Glass. No, there ain't no horrid snakes in this part of the orchard, and if they were, they're as harmless as robins.

# CHAPTER IX.

### CARRIE'S "BOSTON" STORY — "DOT."

I have a story of a little musician, friends. We have lovely music in Boston: I will try to picture it to you.

The church was vast and dim. The air was fragrant with pine boughs, and over the golden cross of the chancel hung heavy wreaths of box and fir. A solitary light shone in front of the organ.

Little feet were heard on the stairs leading to the orchestra. A door in the organ-case opened quietly and was about to close, when a voice was heard:

"Is that you, Dot?" asked the organist.

"Yes, sir."

"What makes you come so early? It is nearly an hour before the rehearsal begins. I should think the little bellows-room would be a rather lonely place to wait an hour."

"I always come early," said the boy, timidly.

"So I have noticed. Why?"

"Mother thinks it best."

"Come out here, and let me talk with you. I have sung in the choir nearly a year, and have hardly had a glimpse of you yet. Don't be bashful! Why, all the music would stop if it were not for you, Dot. Our grandest Christmas anthem would break into confusion if you were to cease to *blow*. Come here. I have just arrived in the city, and have come to the church to wait for the hour of rehearsal. I want company. Come, Dot."

The little side door of the organ moved: a shadow crept along in the dim light towards the genial-hearted tenor.

"Do you like music, Dot?"

"Yes, sir."

"Is that what makes you come so long before the rest?"

"No, sir."

"What is it, then?"

"I have a reason — mother would not like to have me speak of it."

"Do you sing?"

"Yes, at home."

"What do you sing?"

"The parts I hear you sing."

"Tenor, then?"

"Yes."

"Will you sing for me?"

"Now?"

"Yes."

"I will sing '*Hark, what mean?*'"

"Rossini — an adaptation from *Cujus Animam.*"

The boy did not understand.

"Well," said the tenor, "I beat time — now, Dot."

A flute-like voice floated out into the empty edifice, silvery, pure, rising and falling through all the melodious measures of that almost seraphic melody. The tenor leaped to his feet, and stood like one entranced. The voice fell in wavy cadences: "*Heavenly Hallelujahs rise.*" Then it rose, clear as a skylark, with the soul of inspiration in it:

> "Hear them tell that sacred story,
> Hear them chant —"

The tenor, with a nervous motion, turned on the gas-light.

The boy seemed affrighted, and shrank away towards the little door that led to the bellows-room.

"Boy!"

"Sir?"

"There is a fortune in that voice of yours."

"Thank you, sir."

"What makes you hide behind that bench?"

"You won't tell, sir?"

"No: I will befriend any boy with a voice like *that*."

The boy approached the singer and stood beside him.

He said not a word, but only looked toward his feet.

The tenor's eyes followed the boy's.

He saw it all, but he only said tenderly:

"Dot!"

A chancel door opened. An acolyte came in, bearing a long gas-lighter: he touched the chandeliers and they burst into flame. The cross glimmered upon the wall under the Christmas wreaths; the alabaster font revealed its beautiful decorations of calla lilies and smilax; the organ glowed with its tall pipes, and carvings, and cherubs.

The first flash of light in the chancel found Dot hidden in his little room, with the door fast closed behind him.

What a strange place it was! A dim light fell through the open carvings of the organ case.

Great wooden pipes towered aloft, with black mouths — like dragons. Far, far above in the arch was a cherub, without a body — a golden face with purple wings. Dot had looked at it for hours, and wondered.

He sat looking at it to-night with a sorrowful face. There were other footsteps in the church, sounds of light, happy voices.

Presently the bell tinkled. The organist was on his bench. Dot grasped the great wooden handle; it moved up and down, up and down, and then the tall wooden pipes with the dragon mouths began to thunder around him. Then the chorus burst into a glorious strain, which Dot the year before had heard the organist say was the "Midnight Mass of the Middle Ages:"

> "Adeste fideles
> Laeti triumphantes,
> Venite,
> Venite,
> In Bethlehem!"

The great pipes close at hand cease to thunder. The music seemed to run far away into distance, low, sweet and shadowy. There were sympathetic solos and tremulous chords. Then the tempest seemed to come back again, and the luminous arch over the organ sent back into the empty church the jubilant chorus :

> "Venite adoremus,
> Venite adoremus,
> Venite adoremus,
> Dominum."

After the anthem there were solos. The tenor sang one of them, and Dot tried to listen to it as he moved the handle up and down. How sweet it sounded to Dot's ears! It came from a friendly heart — except his mother's it was the only voice that had ever spoken a word of sympathy or praise to the poor bellows-boy.

The singers rested, laughed and talked. Dot listened as usual in his narrow room.

"I came to the church directly from the train," said the tenor, "and amused myself for a time with Dot. A wonderful voice that boy has."

"Dot?" said the precentor.

"Yes; the boy that blows the organ."

"Oh, yes; I had forgotten. I seldom see him," said the precentor. "Now I think of it, the sexton told me some weeks ago that I must get a new organ-boy another year; he says this one — Dot you call him? — comes to the church through back alleys, and goes to the bellows-room as soon as the church is open and hides there until service time, and that his clothes are not decent to be seen in a church on Sunday. Next Sunday begins the year — I must see to the matter."

"He does his work well?" asked the alto, with a touch of sympathy in her voice.

"Yes."

"Would it not be better to get him some new clothes, than to dismiss him?" she asked.

"No. Charity is charity, and business is business. Everything must be first class here. We cannot have ragamuffins creeping into the church to do church work. Of course, I should be glad to have the boy supplied with clothes. That is another thing. But we must have a different person in the bellows-box. The sexton's son is bright, dresses well, and I have no doubt would be glad of the place — Now we will sing the anthem, '*Good-will to men.*'"

The choir and chorus arose. The organist tinkled the bell, and bent down on the pedals and keys. There was a ripple of music, a succession of short sounds, and silence.

The organist touched the knob at the side of the key-board, and again the bell tinkled. His white hands ran over the keys, but there issued no sound.

He moved nervously from the bench, and opened the little door.

"Dot?"

No answer.

"The boy is sick or faint."

The tenor stepped into the room and brought out a limp figure.

"Are you sick, Dot?"

"Yes, sir; what will become of mother?"

"He heard what you said about dismissing him," said the alto to the precentor.

"Yes, but the sexton was right. Look at his shoes — why, his toes are sticking through them."

"And this bitter weather!" said the alto, feelingly.

"Can you blow, Dot?"

"No, sir; it is all dark, sir. I can't see, sir. I can't but just stand up, sir. You won't dimiss me, sir, mother is lame and poor, sir — paralyzed, sir; that's what they call it — can't use but one hand, sir."

"This ends the rehearsal," said the precentor in an impatient way. "Dot, you needn't come tomorrow, nor till I send for you. Here's a dollar, Dot — charity — Christmas present."

One by one the singers went out, the precentor

bidding the sexton have a care that Dot was sent home.

The alto and the tenor lingered. Dot was recovering.

"I shall not hear the music to-morrow. I do love it so."

"You poor child, you shall have your Christmas music to-morrow, and the best the city affords. Do you know where Music Hall is, Dot?"

"Yes, lady."

"There is to be an oratorio there to-morrow evening — *The Messiah*. It is the grandest ever composed, and no singing in America is equal to it. There is one chorus called the 'Hallelujah Chorus' — it is wonderful: the man who composed it thought he heard the angels singing and saw the Lord of Heaven, when he was at work upon it; and *he* is to be the first tenor singer — and *I* am to sing the altos — wouldn't you like to go, Dot?"

"Yes, lady. Is the man who composed it to be the tenor singer — the one who heard the angels singing, and thought he saw the Lord?"

"No, Dot; *he* is to be the tenor singer."

"*I*, Dot," said the tenor.

"I have a ticket for the upper gallery, which I

will give him," said the alto. "A friend of mine bought it, but I gave her a seat on the floor, and kept this for — well, for Dot."

The tenor talked low with the lady.

"Here is a Christmas present, Dot." He handed Dot a bill.

"And here is one for your mother," said the alto, giving Dot a little roll of money.

Dot was better now. He looked bewildered at his new fortune.

"Thank you, lady. Thank you, sir. Are you able?" The alto laughed.

"Yes, Dot. I am to receive a hundred dollars for singing to-morrow evening. I shall try to think of you, Dot, when I am rendering one of the passages — perhaps it will give me inspiration, I shall see you, Dot — under the statue of Apollo."

The sexton was turning off the lights in the chancel. He called Dot. The church grew dimmer and dimmer, and the great organ faded away in the darkness. In the vanishing lights the alto and tenor went out of the church, leaving Dot with the sexton.

It was Sabbath evening — Christmas.

Lights glimmered thickly among the snowy trees

on the Common; beautiful coaches were rolling through the crowded streets.

Dot entered Music Hall timidly by a long passage, through which bright, happy faces were passing, silks rustling, aged people moving sedately and slowly, and into which the crowds on the street seemed surging like a tide. Faces were too eager with expectation to notice him or his feet. At last he passed a sharp angle in the long passage, and the great organ under a thousand gas-jets, burst upon his view. An usher at one of the many lower doors looked at his ticket doubtfully: —

"Second gallery — back."

Dot followed the trailing silks up the broad flights of stairs, reached the top, and asked another usher to show him his seat. The young man whom Dot addressed had that innate refinement of feeling that marks a true Boston gentleman. He gave Dot a smile, as much as to say "I am glad *you* can enjoy all this happiness with the rest," and said: —

"Follow me."

His manner was so kind that Dot thought he would like to speak to him again. He remembered what the alto had said about the statue of

Apollo, and as the usher gave him back his check and pointed to the number on the check and the seat, Dot said:

"Will you please tell me, sir, which is the statue of Apollo?"

The usher glanced at the busts and statues along the wall. He spoke kindly:

"*That* is the Apollo Belvidere."

Dot thought that a pretty name; it did not convey to his mind any association of the Vatican palace, but he knew that some beautiful mystery was connected with it.

And now Dot gazes in amazement on the scene before him. In the blaze of light the great organ rises resplendently, sixty feet in height, its imposing façade hiding from view its six thousand pipes. People are hurrying into the hall, flitting to and fro; young ladies in black silks and velvets and satins; old men — where were so many men with white hair ever seen before? stately men with thin faces, bald — teachers, college professors. Tiers of seats in the form of half a pyramid rise at either end of the organ. These are filling with the chorus — sopranos and altos in black dresses, and white shawls, tenors and basses in black coats, white neck-ties and kids. In front, between the great chorus, rises a dark statue, and around this musicians are gathering — players on violins, violas, violoncellos, contra basses, flutes, oboes, bassoons, trumpets, trombones, horns; the pyramidal seats fill; the hall overflows; the doors are full, the galleries. The instruments tune. A dark-haired man steps upon the conductor's stand; he raises his baton; there is a hush, then half a hundred instruments pour forth the symphony.

Dot listens. He has never heard such music before; he did not know that anything like it was ever heard on earth. It grows sweeter and sweeter: —

"Comfort ye."

Did an angel speak? The instruments are sweeter now: —

"Comfort ye my people."

Did that voice come from the air?

Dot listens and wonders if this is earth: —

"Comfort ye, comfort ye my people, saith your God, saith your God."

Dot sees a tall man standing alone — in front of the musicians — is it he that is singing? Dot gazes upon his face with wide eyes. It is *he*—

and *he* is the tenor who had befriended him the night before.

What music followed when the chorus arose and sang : —

"Every valley shall be exalted!"

Dot hears the grand music sweep on, and he feels, as all feel, that the glorious Messiah is about to appear. He sees a lady in white satin and flashing jewels step forward : he hears a ripple of applause, and a voice full of strength and feeling sings :

"Oh thou that tellest good tidings to Zion. O thou that tellest good tidings to Jerusalem, say unto the cities of Judah, Behold your God!"

Dot knows that voice. Will indeed she lift her eyes to him?

No, she does not. She sits down, the hall ringing with applause. She rises, bows, but she does not look towards the statue of Apollo, near which Dot is sitting.

Dot hears dreamy music now, more enchanting than any before it. The great audience do not stir, or move a fan, or raise a glass. It grows more ethereal; it seems now but a wavy motion in the air. He hears a lady near whisper: —

"The pastoral symphony."

The alto has risen again. She stands out from the great chorus — what a beautiful figure! The dark-haired man lifts his baton : the lady turns her face toward the upper gallery. Her eyes wander for a moment ; they rest on — Dot :

> He shall feed his flock like a shepherd, and he shall gather the lambs with his arm, and carry them in his bosom, and gently lead those that are with young.

There was no applause now. Tears stood in the alto's eyes — tears stood in the eyes of every one. There was a deep hush, and tears, and in the silence the alto stood looking steadily at — Dot.

There was a rustle in the hall — it grew. The silence was followed by a commotion that seemed to rock the hall. The applause gathered force like a tempest.

Then the beautiful lady looked towards Dot, and sang again the same wonderful air, and all the hall grew still, and people's eyes were wet again.

The Hallelujah Chorus with its grand fugues was sung, the people rising and standing with bowed heads during the majestic outpouring of praise.

It is ended now — faded and gone. The great organ stands silent in the dark hall ; the coaches have rolled away, the clocks are striking midnight.

"I have come to congratulate you before retiring," said our tenor to the alto, as he stepped into the parlor of the Revere House. "To-night has been the triumph of your life. Nothing so moved the audience as "*He shall feed his flock like a shepherd.*"

"Do you know to what I owed the feeling that so inspired me in that air?"

"No."

"It was poor little Dot in the gallery. You teach music, do you not?"

"Yes."

"You are about to open a school?"

"Yes."

"Give Dot a place as office boy — errand boy — something. It will lift a weight from my heart.

"I had thought of it. He has a beautiful voice."

"I might get him a place in a choir."

Fifteen years have passed. The old Handel and Haydn Society have sung *The Messiah* fifty, perhaps sixty times. The snows of December are again on the hills. The grand oratorio is again rehearsing for the Sabbath evening before Christmas.

A new tenor is to sing on the occasion—he was born in Boston, has studied in Milan, and has achieved great triumphs as an interpreter of sacred music in London and Berlin.

The old hall is filled again. The symphony has begun its dulcet enchantment; the Tenor, with a face luminous and spiritual, arises, and with his first notes thrills the audience and holds it as by a spell:—

"Comfort ye."

He thought of the time when he first heard those words. He thought of the hearts whose kindness had made him a singer. Where were they? Their voices had vanished from the choirs of earth, but in spirit those sweet singers seemed hovering around him:—

"Comfort ye my people."

He looked, too, towards the Apollo on the wall. He recalled the limp bellows-boy who had sat there sixteen years ago. How those words then comforted him! How he loved to sing them now!

"Speak ye comfortably to Jerusalem, and cry unto her that her warfare is accomplished, that her iniquity is pardoned."

It was Dot.

# CHAPTER X.

REV. MR. GLASS MAKES A CLAM-BAKE FOR HIS CITY FRIENDS, WITH RESULTS DESCRIBED BY AUNT TO UNCLE AS FOLLOWS:

" Eben, is that you?

" I'm glad you have come home. Such a day as I have had!

" *Why?* Mr. Glass's clam-bake.

" Mr. Glass! — he hasn't any more brains than a robin — I don't like him, and I don't believe Jefferson does, either. I'd like to hear him preach just once. I suppose I shall when I go up from the Cape.

" *What has happened?* What ain't happened! Mr. Glass, you know, was so taken with that clambake that we had here last week, that he thought it would be a very fine notion to give a bake of his own to his Boston friends. You told him that you had no objection, and on Carrie's account I favored the plan. I rather wanted to see his Boston friends. Well, he hired Hoggarty, the

Irishman, to help him; also counted on the help of Jeff.

"Well, you ought to have seen his friends as they came skippin' up to the house after the train arrived! They were a lot of young men, thin as rails. Some on them had spectacles on one eye and some on both; all had canes or umbrellas, and books or magazines.

"Mr. Glass ran out to meet um, and I heard one on um say:

"'How are ye, old boy?' We don't meet our minister in that way.

"There were eight on um. In the course of an hour, I happened to look out of the window, and I saw a sight that would have astonished one of the old prophets. It was two objects flying through the air, half men and half wheels; like the pictures in the almanac, of a strange race of beings in early times, half men and half horses. The wheel seemed flying the men, and where the man left off and the wheel began I couldn't imagine.

" Up they came to the door.

"Brought our *centipedes* with us, old fellow," said one of them to Mr. Glass. "Been making the sand fly for an hour."

"Then the men and the wheels came apart. I never was more astonished in my life.

"Mr. Glass had bought ten bushels of clams to feed these ten young men. Why, ten bushels would have fed a thousand such fellows, with basket *fulls* to spare.

"There was a great smoke at the bake-hole; Mr. Glass and Mr. Hoggarty ran hither and thither. I was very busy makin' the dressin' and the pies, and Carrie entertained the ten thin young men on the piazza.

"About one o'clock Jeff came in with a scared look on his face.

"'Somethin' happened,' said he.

"'Massy! What?' said I.

"'The bake-hole is opened, and Hoggarty has run away.'

"'Hoggarty's run away?'

"'Yes, he opened the bake-hole, and ate one or two clams, and just said "Holy St. Patrick!" and leaped over the wall and run home a minute, and I have just seen him going over the hill half a mile away. What do you suppose it is?'

"'Luny, I guess,' said I.

"'What's to be done?'

"'I'll tell you. You act as waiter; bring the bake to the tables, and I will go out and serve it at the tables. That will make things pleasant all around.'

HAGGARTY RUNS.

"When I went to the tables there sot the ten young men lookin' as though they hadn't had anything to eat since childhood. As I remarked, some on um had spectacles on one eye, and some on both. Mr. Glass and Carrie sat at the head of the table.

"'The bake is ready,' said I.

"'Yes,' said Mr. Glass. 'The waiter has gone; queer, aint it?'

"'I have arranged with Jeff to serve the tables. Will you ask a blessin', Mr. Glass?'

"He turned white as a ghost and then red as a rooster, and there followed a strange sort of a silence — and he a minister, too! I couldn't imagine what made him so backward, none of the Cape ministers are so. *We* always ask a blessing at a clam-bake.

"I was determined to stand by my colors. I never yet feared the face of clay. I covered my face with my hands, and made up my mind that I wouldn't move an inch until Mr. Glass or one of those students, asked a blessin'.

"It was awful solemn.

"Well, while I was in that devotional attitude, waitin', Hoggarty's wife came up behind me unbeknown, and fairly hissed in my ear:—

"'That there bake is all *raw*! Just as raw as 'twas when it went into the bake-hole. That city feller made the bake-hole of *old* stones.'

"It came upon me like a thunder-clap!

"'Pity sake! where *is* Hoggarty?' said I in a whisper.

"'He's *scooted* — he wa'n't to blame.'

"Well I got up and went to the bake-hole, and just bit one of those clams, and it was just as tough as whit-leather. I turned round and rolled my eyes up to the skies.

"There's nothin' like havin' grace at a tryin' time. You think that I havn't much self-control; but I have. I felt as though I wished that the earth would open and swaller me up; but when I looked around and saw the wonderin' look on Mr. Glass's face, and Carrie dressed up so pretty, and lookin' so innocent, I just said :—

"'The bake is not quite ready yet; if you will all go to the croquet-ground for an hour or so, Jeff and I will arrange it, and I will call you when we are ready.'

"Then I took a peck of them clams out of the ten bushel in the bake-hole, and boiled um quick over the kitchen fire, and I served them with all the good things in the house, and when they had all had a good dinner and a good time, I asked 'em if one of 'em wouldn't return thanks — and who do you think did it?

"Jeff?"

"Yes, Jeff, and I never was more astonished in all my life. But, then, Jeff was the only one besides myself who really knew how much there was to be thankful for.

"Well, I did everything I could to make the visit pleasant and to cover up the ignorance of Mr. Glass, and just as one of them centipede men was hoppin' onto his wheel, what do you suppose I heard him say to Mr. Glass? — Just this: —

"'You didn't fix that bake right, old fellow, and if it hadn't been for Old Mother Sassafras, we wouldn't have had any dinner at all.'

"'Old Mother Sassafras!' And that after all I had done for them, too!"

## CHAPTER XI.

#### THE OLD HOUSE AND HOME, AND AUNT DESIRE'S TWO WISHES.

There is a charm about an old country house, if its associations have been interesting. Uncle Eben's was older than the Republic, and a part of its mahogany furniture had come far down from colonial times. In the old parlor, his ancestors for three generations had been married. In one of the great chambers, called the "spare chamber" his grand-parents, great-grand-parents, and several uncles and aunts, of saintly memory, had died.

In this last room were portraits, old family Bibles, hymn books, silhouettes and "samplers." Over the open fire-place, from whose hearth the old-time log-fires had now forever faded, was a cupboard or recess containing the Family Christian Library, Edward's works, the *American Magazine*, the New England *Family Magazine* and the *Youth's Companion*. On an antique bureau were copies of the old English poets — Collins, Gray, Beattie, Thompson, Goldsmith.

I read here these fine old pastoral poets, with appreciation, for the first time. Their influence fostered my growing taste for the independency of country living and thinking; they led me to see rural life as I had never interpreted it before.

Aunt Desire was a wonderful house-keeper; she was in more respects than one a superior woman, with all her eccentricities.

"I should be perfectly happy," said uncle to me confidentially one day, "if it were not for wife's tongue. But then," he added, "she took such good care of my father and mother and aunts in their old age; that was when she was a young woman, too. Why, there were ten years that she did not go out anywhere; just devoted herself to my folks as though they had been her own. That is what I call a test of love.

"She will never see the money, poor woman, that she let Dr. Gamm have to invest." He added with a half roguish look, " Won't her tongue go when she finds out how she has been taken in? But I have two hundred dollars that I can spare, and I am going to give her that when she goes up from the Cape. She will be a wiser woman before she returns."

The table was always kept set, and was loaded with the best food at breakfast, dinner and tea. The new milk, fresh eggs, vegetables of all kinds direct from the garden, the honey, preserves, and berries, were my choice, although Aunt said that I seldom ate anything but the "trimmin's of the table."

There was a spirit of fine old hospitality in thus keeping the table always ready for the guest. In spring and fall the drovers used to call and be entertained. In mid-summer, Methodist ministers and class-leaders, especially of the old school, frequently stopped on their way to the vineyard.

There was a "prophet's chamber" kept especially for brethren who liked to prolong their stay, an occurrence that was not uncommon.

It was a somewhat remarkable room, this "prophet's chamber." The bedstead had high posts, curiously carved, and curtains. Over the shelf hung a steel engraving of the death of John Wesley. Biographies of Zinzendorf, Wesley, Fenelon, Madam Guyon, and of several notable revivalists of the last century were piled upon the table. The woodbine fell loosely about the windows, and the swallows above it made their nests in the eaves.

The interest that uncle took in me seemed

rather remarkable after the indifference with which I had been treated at home. Father was always absorbed in business, and mother in society. My brothers were never intimate with each other, but made their friendships outside of the family.

Uncle never, or seldom, gave me advice directly. When he wished to show me a truth, and impress it upon me, he commonly did it by illustration.

I had told him that my love of billiard playing had sometimes led me to the bar, that I might not seem discourteous to those who invited me to such refreshments. I noticed that his face always shadowed when I made allusion to these conventionalities; he seemed to indicate by his manner that he thought it dangerous not to be always positive and strong. I shall never forget, how one evening, he expressed this thought to me.

We were sitting under the porch woodbine, uncle and aunt, sister and I. Aunt chanced to speak of Stephen Marliave, a man of some local reputation, who had died within a year.

"Yes — Stephen," said uncle. "He was one of the largest-hearted men I ever knew. We all owed something to Stephen."

Then he added in a tone of regret: —

"He had only one fault."

The light fell in pencil rays through the trees. I sat in silence enjoying the refreshing coolness.

"He had great abilities, Stephen had. We sent him to the Legislature three times. They thought of nominating him for Governor.

"But," he added, sadly, "Stephen had one fault." He looked at me.

I made no answer. I was tired.

"A very generous man, Stephen was. Always visited the sick — he was feeling — when any one was in trouble. The old people all liked him. Even the children used to follow him in the streets."

"A good man, indeed," I said, indifferently.

"Yes; he only had one fault."

"What was that?" I asked.

"Only intemperance."

"Did it harm him?"

"Yes, somewhat. He didn't seem to have any power to resist it at last. He got behindhand and had to mortgage his farm, and finally had to sell it. His wife died on account of the reverse; kind of crushed, disappointed. Then his children, not having the right bringing up, turned out badly. His intemperance seemed to mortify them and take away their spirit. He had to leave politics; 'twouldn't do, you see. Then we had to set him aside from church, and at last his habits brought on paralysis and we had to take him to the poor-house. He died there; only forty-five. There were none of his children at the funeral. Poor man, he had only one fault.

"Only one fault!" He paused.

"The ship had only one leak, but it went down.

"Only one fault!" He paused again.

"The temple had only one decaying pillar, but it fell.

"Only one fault. Home gone, wife lost, family ruined, honor forfeited, social and religious privileges abandoned; broken health, poverty, paralysis and the poorhouse.

"One fault, only one, Jefferson.

"Stephen had but *one* fault."

I said nothing. He added: —

"Indulgence in a single wrong propensity, no matter how small it may seem at first, is an open way to ruin. The loss of some of the finest characters that the world has seen may be traced to a single fault, as some of the most stately wrecks that drift upon the seashore are caused by a single imperfect timber."

> 'Men
> Carrying, I say, the stamp of one defect,
> Their virtues else be they as pure as grace,
> As infinite as man may undergo,
> Shall in the general censure take corruption
> From that particular fault.'

"A single error destroys one's self respect, weakens one's resolution, and impairs one's confidence in God. The knowledge of evil is a fearful thing, and the only safety for a youth is to resist its beginnings; for 'the beginning of evil is as when one letteth out water.'"

I saw the truth that he wished to convey, and felt it.

He was not only careful for my moral training, but seemed concerned about a matter with which I had never been approached before — my political opinions and education.

"I tried to bring my sons up well," he remarked, the same evening, "and I put in their way the best books on American history — I wanted them to know how to vote. Every American young man should be trained to vote intelligently. I hope brother is thoughtful about this matter?"

"Father?"

"Yes."

"Why he never votes himself. Says he has no time."

"And Eugene?"

"Brother Eugene — he says it is vulgar to vote; that no gentlemen's sons now take any interest in American politics. He belongs to a swell club; young men who talk *English* politics; read the *London Athenæum* and *N. Y. National;* — pride themselves on knowing nothing about home affairs at all. Why, I don't think Eugene could tell who is his representative in Congress."

"Now, Eben," said Aunt, "why do you set that boy to talkin' in that way. Eugene Endicott is a gentleman, and don't hang around town meetin's as our boys used to do. Perhaps if you sent your sons to Paris, after they had left the Academy, they never would have gone West. I always had an ambition for those boys. You meant well — but it ain't no use to say nothin'. There ain't much for any on us in this world."

She rocked violently to and fro, and added: —

"What would I give if those boys were here to-night. I wish that they had never gone away. It was nothing but that independent spirit that Eben *distilled* into them, that sent them off West. John went to Kansas that he might vote the Free State ticket at the time of the struggle against the Lecompton Constitution; how I do hate that word; I used to hear nothing else in Old Buchanan's times. Then Henry followed him, and both came near being killed by the Border Ruffians, as they called them. It was my prayer that one of them boys might become a lawyer and the other a minister. I would have felt that I had lived for something then. Those were the two wishes that I used to carry to the Lord — but 'twan't no use to carry 'em to the Lord, and tain't no use to say nothin' — you all know what husband is, you know."

## CHAPTER XII.

### THE OLD CAMP-MEETING AND THE NEW.

"Who do you think is goin' to preach on the camp-ground, Sunday?" asked Aunt Desire, of Uncle, one August day, laying down the paper.

"The Bishop?"

"No."

"Dr. Hope?"

"No."

"I do not know."

"Dr. Gamm. I'm goin."

There was a bright expression in Aunt's face, and a shadowy one in Uncle's.

"I don't think that I will attend," said Uncle.

"Then I will git Jeff to go with me."

Uncle looked relieved.

I had heard Uncle's friends who were Methodists, relate wonderful tales of the old-time Vineyard Camp-Meeting, now a by-gone glory. The patriarchal simplicity of these gatherings of God, beneath the great oaks through which continually breathed the summer winds of the sea, was indeed a holy memory to the old, and the picture has a poetic charm for any susceptible and devout mind, and although I well knew that the camp-meetings of to-day were too much exhibitions of vulgar wealth and pleasure seeking, I could hardly divest them of the coloring of their old associations.

What scenes were these old gatherings like the school of prophets, under the oaks! The camp of tents arose like the tents of the Hebrews around the early tabernacle. There multitudes gathered to listen to men moved by the Divine Spirit, and to seek the securities of that life that shall out-live the stars. We are told of the "shining countenances of Christian faces lighted up with holy joy:" of the morning songs in the tents as the great sun stood like a gate of fire half risen above the sea; of the sunrise hymn of the new converts, which was termed in mystic language, "The serenade of angels." Father Bonny was there: Kent, Butler, Allen, Liversey. We hear the old Methodist speak of the "awful sense of the Divine Presence" that used to fill the encampment; how that, to use the highly mystical terms of the period, "the slain of the Lord lay upon every side."

We are told of Sabbath mornings that rose

"amid bursts of hallelujahs from the hosts of the Spiritual Israel;" of the parting ceremonies, when the people, marching in a procession, within the circle of the tents, suddenly halted, and then each passing all the others, bid every one a farewell.

> " Farewell, my dear brethren, the time is at hand,
> That we must be parted from this social band. "

What serene days were those when the midsummer sunlight in the dry heaven dreamed over the great water ways to the ocean : How awful was the scene when the tempest darkened the red sky, and smote the sea, and bent before it the giant oaks: How calmly and gloriously rose the full moon when the tempest had passed : What hymns arose in the grove — prophets' inspirations, and not mocking birds' songs. I seem to hear them, as the old people used to sing them to me in childhood, on my visits to Sandwich and Falmouth.

It was holy ground. Where easy preachers now too often blow the bubbles of poetic speculation, and lighter hearers as often listen, dividing their time, perhaps, between pulpit pyrotechnics and those of another kind; where showy peddlers of real estate talk over their wares, and look out on the sea and up to the stars of the sky and hold both as mere pieces of valueless property, the bushes once burned with flame, and the altars of Jehovah blazed with celestial fire.

We went to the Camp-Meeting — aunt and I.

If the "Old Spirit" was gone, the beautiful temple of nature remained, even with the deformities of the hotels and the cottages of the spiritual sluggards that surrounded it. The old groves I wished to see, the star-light over the waters, the sunrise, the summer bays with their thousand sails, all brought back the stories I had heard of the time when here simple souls came together to worship God in spirit and in truth.

Such people came here now : they were respected as "old time Methodists," but their power with people was gone. The Vineyard Association could no longer say, "silver and gold have I none," nor to the helpless halting soul, "rise up and walk." Uncle had described the change to me, and I saw it as he saw it, and as any one may see it at a glance, as his eye sweeps the gay town of the trees.

We arrived Saturday evening. Aunt's first inquiry of the brethren was for the "boardin' place of Rev. Dr. Gamm."

"I have some secular business with him," she said to me, when she noticed my surprise. "My dividends — you know; I told you."

The next day was in August splendor. There was a brilliant gathering of unconcerned-looking people in the pavilion. Dr. Gamm preached on electricity and the velocity of celestial visitants to the earth; the inter-stellar wonders, and the city of gold. It was a meteor flash; a surprise, and gone.

When he ended, Aunt hastened to the platform, which was filled with ministers. The Doctor evidently saw her coming, and did not desire an interview, and quickly moved away with one of his friends.

After the evening sermon, which was given by a holy-looking, spiritual-minded old man, and was of excellent spirit and influence, a social meeting was held, and among the leaders appeared the Doctor. Aunt also appeared, an unexpected seeker after knowledge, and presently the Doctor had gone.

"I didn't enjoy the meetin' greatly," said Aunt to me, after the service was over; "never mind; I'll have it out with Dr. Gamm when I come up from the Cape. I'll show him my *capabilities* yet — you wait and see."

The old man's evening sermon, as I said, was beautiful. It made me feel that there was something in his soul that I needed to complete my life and its aim and happiness that I did not possess. I dreamed of it.

The next day, as we steamed away on the pretty boat, several people on deck discussed the Sunday morning sermon in our hearing.

"A fine discourse, that on the inter-stellar wonders and celestial splendors," said one.

"Reminded me of Daniel or Ezekiel's vision," said another.

"Like the descent of the gods on Olympus," said a pretty miss.

"Of what did it remind you?" I asked of Aunt Desire.

"Well, Jeff, I was rather worldly-minded, yesterday. It reminded me, well — I wouldn't like to say."

"Just to me?"

"Well — Treasure Mountain. Don't tell Eben. You know what husband is, you know."

# CHAPTER XIII.

PICNICS. — "CROWS IN THE TREES AND HAWKS IN THE AIR."

On one of the hills back of the orchard, called Pine Tree Hill, was an old Indian burial-ground, such as are often seen on the farms near the coast. It was shaded by a grove of pines and oaks; the ground was full of sea-shells, and the graves were marked by rows of mossy stones, whose tops had almost sunk to a level with the grass.

It was a favorite picnic-ground. Parties, societies and churches held picnics there, in much the same way that church societies made their annual clam-bakes under the fifty-year-old trees in the orchard.

I sometimes went there with uncle, on warm afternoons, the better to enjoy the breeze from the Bay. Uncle liked the place, and sometimes read old histories there, under the trees.

He told me there many Indian stories that are

not found in histories, as he said, but which he thought very romantic and of much local interest. Among these were accounts of Alexander, the son of the great Massasoit, and his warrior queen, Weebamo, who was truly a Boadicea; of the son of Philip who was sold into slavery to Spain; of Amy, the daughter of Massasoit, whose descendants still live in a town above the Cape, and are sometimes called " The Princesses."

Whenever the children had a picnic on Pine Tree Hill, they invited Aunt Desire. Her stories and her cookies, as well as many friendly offices in the way of dishes, pitchers of milk, and pitchers of water, were sure to be a benevolent feature of the rustic spread. Aunt was a kind of gypsy queen on such occasions ; a delight to all good people and obedient children, and a terror to evil doers ; her opinions were decisive, and her influence over the young was absolute. A hundred questions arise at such a gathering, but no one ever thought of disputing the opinions and decisions of Aunt Desire.

Sitting on the grass or carpet of dry pine needles, under the intermingling trees, with one or two old ladies, and a dozen or some twenty children about her, what delightful stories she used to tell! There was a kind of magic and magnetism in them, or rather perhaps in her manner of telling them, that spirited the youthful fancy off to fairy-land. One of these stories, often repeated, related to a certain wild goose which an old wife on the Cape once gave to her son to carry to sea for his Thanksgiving dinner, but which flew home after a voyage of some days, and was found in the farm-yard, "*honking*," on Thanksgiving morning.

But her favorite story with the little people, she called "Crows in the Trees and Hawks in the Air." I heard her relate it several times. She gave it an air of mystery, and imitated the birds of which she spoke with highly dramatic effect, and made the final tragedy wonderfully agreeable to the children by liberal donations of cookies.

### CROWS IN THE TREES AND HAWKS IN THE AIR.

"It is a story with a moral," she would begin. "*Have some cookies?* Now, listen, and you will learn what it is not to obey your betters. 'Tis a dreadful thing, a very dreadful thing. There are crows in the trees and hawks in the air. Let me tell you about Biddy High-Fly.

"Well, old Mrs. Red Comb was a very discreet bird, but she had a very ambitious pullet, who had caused her more trouble than all the rest of her brood. The pullet's name was Miss High-Fly.

"'My daughter,' said Mrs. Red Comb to her one day, 'I am afraid that you will come to some evil end. There are crows in the trees and hawks in the air. Your waywardness troubles me. Let me advise you to be on very obedient terms with the mistress of the farm-house. Let her make your nest and select your eggs for setting, and have the oversight of your family when they are hatched.'

"'Not I,' said Biddy High-Fly. 'Not I. Cut —cut—cut—not I, cut! They don't rob me of half of my eggs, and then stick me up in a dingy hen-house on the same nest in which my great grandmother used to sit. I'm a biddy of spirit, I be—cut—cut—a cut! I mean to steal my nest in the woods or fields, and have all of my eggs myself, I do. Then I shall come home at last bringing a brood that will make all of the hens cackle, and the mistress of the farm-house stare.'

"'But the crows?'

"'A straw for the crows! I will hide my nest.'

"'And the hawks?'

"'A fly for the hawks! They'll find that there is one biddy that has the courage to defend herself.'

"'What would you do with your chickens after they were hatched? Who would feed them?'

"'Squire Parsnip's corn-field would be good picking, I fancy.'

"'The squire's men would kill you.'

"'They'd have to catch me first. I have got both legs and wings, I have. I should squat down if I heard any one coming.'

"Mrs. Red Comb dropped her tail in despair, and only said, 'You poor, silly creature! You will find out one day that there are crows in the trees and hawks in the air!'

"So Biddy High-Fly made her a nest under a bramble-bush in the woods. She laid sixteen eggs, and then she begun to sit.

"One sunny afternoon she was startled by the sound of 'caw — caw — caw,' and presently Mr. Crow dropped down on a green bough near her nest. Biddy's heart was all a-flutter.

"'Fine afternoon,' said Mr. Crow — 'caw — caw caw.'

"'Yes, sir, — cut — cut,' answered Biddy, very short.

"'You are one of the finest biddies I ever saw,' said Mr. Crow. 'You have a nice nest of eggs, no doubt?'

"'Cut—a—cut,' said Biddy, good-humoredly, smoothing her ruffled feathers.

"'Will you just rise a little, and let me see your fine eggs?' politely asked Mr. Crow.

"Biddy displayed her treasures.

"'If you hatch all of those fine eggs,' said Mr. Crow, 'you and your family will be the ornament and glory of the woods. I wish you success. Good-afternoon. I will call again some day.'

"Mr. Crow bowed very politely, and Biddy, feeling highly flattered, rose and made a courtesy.

"Mr. Crow did indeed call again one day, and at a time when Biddy was not at home. When she came back to her nest she found that four of her eggs were gone. She concluded that some low-bred pole-cat had been that way, but she never suspected polite Mr. Crow.

"Biddy resolved not to go out of sight of her nest again, but to live by catching flies. She frequently observed Mr. Crow sitting upon the top of a tall maple tree, and wondered that he did not drop down and have a chat.

"*Have some cookies? Now, do; there's more to foller.*

"Well, one day Mr. Crow called again, bringing with him a number of his friends. They complimented Biddy on her beauty, and Mr. Crow, alighting close to her nest, asked her if she wouldn't be so accommodating as to rise and let his friends see her fine eggs.

"Biddy rose very proudly, when suddenly Mr. Crow darted under her, and, lifting her up, gave her a toss over his head. His friends alighted around the nest, and a goodly feast they had.

"When Biddy picked herself up, and saw her eggs disappearing, she begun to scold most lustily.

"'O, you deceitful, lying creature!' she said. 'Cut — cut — a — cut. You black rascal! a — cut. You wicked thief! Cut — a — cut!'

"Presently there was a report of a gun in Squire Parsnip's corn-field, and Mr. Crow and his friends made a rapid exit.

"Biddy found but one egg unbroken, and, with gloomy thoughts, she sat down on that solitary egg, and hid her head under her wing, poor thing.

"In the course of time her one egg hatched, and she started, with her chick, for Squire Parsnip's corn-field. On her way she heard a rustling of wings above her head, and, looking up, saw

Mr. Hawk. She sat down quickly, covering her little chick, and crying : —

"'N-a-a-a!'

"'Yes,' said Mr. Hawk, 'your chicken for my dinner, if you please.'

"'N-a-a-a,' said Biddy, bristling her feathers, so as to look as large and savage as possible.

"Mr. Hawk lit on Biddy's back, and, for a few minutes, made the feathers fly. Biddy couldn't stand this, so, uttering a cry of terror, she flew towards the wall and hid herself under a stone. The last that she heard of her little chick, it was peeping in the sky.

"When she recovered from her fright, she went to Squire Parsnip's corn-field and flew over the wall.

"'Shew!' exclaimed a frightful voice, and poor Biddy flew back again, and ran for the farm-house in the greatest terror.

"'Haw — haw — haw!' laughed Mr. Crow, as he saw Biddy trudging home. 'Haw — haw — haw! What a fright of a hen!' And all the crows on the tree-tops chorussed 'Haw — haw — haw!'

"The hens all laughed and cackled when Biddy returned, for she was poor, and without a chick, and her back was all bare of feathers.

"'There's that missing hen,' said the mistress of the farm-house, to her man, Joe. 'Catch her, and put her in the hen-coop to fat, and we'll kill her some day. She don't look fit to be out of doors.'

"So Biddy High-Fly went into the iron pot, and was never seen again after the dinner that day.

"Now, children, this is a kind of an allegory, as Bunyan would say. Always obey what older people say to ye, because there are crows in the trees and hawks in the air. Always listen to what the preacher says. There are crows in the trees and hawks in the air. And what your teacher says. There are crows in the trees and hawks in the air.

"Don't be scared — not too scared, I mean. Be good, and they'll never get ye. Now we'll have a cookie apiece.

"What is the Scripture moral of that story I told you?"

"There are crows in the trees and hawks in the air," always chorus the children.

"Don't you forget it!"

# CHAPTER XIV.

### TWO LETTERS.

We had been riding over the sandy roads — Uncle and I. We were late for supper, and as we were leaving the table, Aunt said:

"Here is a letter for each of you; I guess yours, Eben, is from the boys."

We went to the piazza, and both of us were soon absorbed in reading the letters we had received.

After reading, we each sat in silence.

Aunt came out for a moment, to ask Eben if the "boys were well," and, being assured that they were, returned to her work.

"This letter," said Uncle, "I hope will prove the first ray of a great joy. It makes me very happy."

"Mine is different," said I. "It seems to me like the shadow of a great sorrow. It makes me sad. It is from father."

"Brother — isn't he well?"

"No."

"May I read it."

"I will read it to you presently. It excites me strangely. Won't you read me yours, Uncle? you say it is pleasant; it will perhaps make me feel easier."

"It is from Henry — marked '*Private*'"

KANSAS CITY,<br>August 22d.

MY DEAR FATHER :—

I am to-day forty-five years old. You will be glad to know that I am successful and prosperous. Whatever I am I owe to the influences of my dear old home on the Cape. It was there I learned the principles that gave me independence of character, and moral and physical strength. I have tried to be true to the principles you were so careful to inculcate, not so much by word as by example. Your influence grows upon me with years — never a son had a better father, and it is because you always were true to your own sense of duty that I have aimed to be true to mine.

When I came to Kansas, it was more from the desire to help make it a free state than to gain wealth or reputation. You know what the influence of the *N. Y. Tribune* was to me then; how your talk of the duties of Americans to the higher law of right fired me. I was willing to fight as I had voted, and to die to make a single state of this nation of great possibilities true to the principles of righteousness and freedom.

I was poor then. I am well-to-do to-day. I have a beautiful home, and a farm of a thousand acres; I have a true wife, and four children to whom I am teaching in religion, in politics, in conduct of life, all that you taught me when I was a boy.

You will ask why I am now writing from Kansas City. I came here to attend a political conference. It may please you to know that I have just been nominated for congress from this district, and I think my prospects of election are good, as the people seem to respect me, and the republicans generally elect their congressmen by a large majority.

Do not tell mother of my nomination. If I were to fail of the election it would grieve her. She used to wish me to study law. If I am elected to congress it will probably as greatly please her as though I had become a lawyer. In the event of my election I will write to her and shall hope to surprise her; so please do not let her see this letter, or be told of this matter if you can prevent it.

It is said that children fulfill the ideals or desires of their mothers. John seems likely to do so. Mother wished him to study for the ministry. Patriotism brought him here. He has done well. He is rich; better, he is a man of good influence. He has been a class leader for five years, and has taken so much interest in the founding of churches and schools in destitute places that he has just been nominated for the presidency of the Western Home Mission Society, which will greatly increase his opportunities for doing good. His influence, were he a minister, would hardly be as great as now. I think his life does credit to his home teachings. It is such lives that have made Kansas, Nebraska, Iowa and Minnesota the New England of the West.

Remember me to dear, faithful mother. Whatever may be my future, be assured of my resolution to be true to my God, my parents, and my country.

Faithfully yours,<br>HENRY ENDICOTT.

"That letter does me good; it is more to me than will be the fact of Henry's election; to be a true man is more than to be a congressman. It makes me feel that I have not lived in vain, notwithstanding the hard things Desire sometimes says to me. But she means well — Desire. Right living will produce right fruit at last, and her eyes will be opened some day. I can wait."

"But brother's letter?"

"I do not understand it — I hope you may. It seems to me dreadful."

BOSTON, August 20th.

JEFFERSON: — You wrote me that you had invited your aunt to come to the city. I wish that you would return and bring her with you. She has strong good sense, and is an excellent nurse. I want some one of strong will near me; it would help me.

I am not well. The doctor says that it was only a slight effusion; that it will soon pass away. I can't sleep; I take chloral, but I can't sleep. My brain is a-flame. The world is wild, and where am I? I am gone, lost!

I shall be calmer to-morrow; to-night I shall walk,

walk! How cool the air will be when the night comes. Darkness! it is cool in the dark. The grave is dark and cool.

It is the fever in my brain that makes me say these things. I shall be calmer to-morrow.

Your mother will remain at Newport late. I would have it so. The crash is coming; let her enjoy life while she can. Don't tell her I am ill. I am not ill. Eugene is at Etretat. He only writes when he wants money. Archie has gone to Long Branch with Stanley.

I have not treated Desire as I ought, wife is so proud and peculiar. You know how it was.

I shall be calmer to-morrow.

Come at once, my dear boy.

I suppress a thousand agonies.

YOUR FATHER.

P. S. I was greatly excited when I wrote the above. The doctor has been here and left me more chloral. He says that there is no cause for alarm. The effusion is only slight. I am calmer now. My business,—oh! my affairs! But I must not think! Destroy this. It will show you my condition if anything were to happen.

# CHAPTER XV.

### AUNT'S FAREWELL EXHORTATION.

That summer on the Cape was the happiest I had known. I think the influence of it will last as long as I live. I certainly hope that Uncle's influence may. He quietly taught me that there is something in life better than I had known, a simple faith in good that has the promises of development beyond this stage of our being, and this lesson I had not as well learned in the city, with all of its scholarship and social advantages.

Every thing charmed me until father's letter brought a shadow. It was a pleasure to be jogged along the country roads in an open carriage. Wild roses and morning glories line the old stone walls in summer, and white, feathery clematis and flaming golden rods in autumn. It is a pleasure to have your own boat and drift along a coast about which no books or Boston letters have been written; to feel that all the delightful things you discover are your own. It is a pleasure to go strawberrying, and blackberrying and whortleberrying, with lunch and pail, and to know that the delicious pies and cakes are made from *your* berries.

The haying season! — the charm of that haying I shall never forget. What is the cropped Boston Public Garden to ten acres of newly cut clover, spread out like a green sea; with the dew dying out of its thousand swaths; with the air heavy with perfume; with an hundred robins and thrushes singing in the locust trees, and bob-o'-links tossing themselves about in the sun!

I had been to church every Sunday during my visit, and such regularity was a new experience to me. I even took a class in the Sunday school, a work for which I had no qualification but uncle's good influence.

During the minister's vacation Uncle took charge of the social meetings, and on such occasions I always went with him.

"Eben is not a powerful exhorter," said Aunt Desire to me one day; "you know what husband is, you know. Still," she further informed me, "what he says in meetin' is generally worth listening to and sometimes it is uncommonly interestin', sort of impresses you, you know."

"Aunt's exhortations were regarded as "powerful." They were certainly energetic and definitive. She held to the old methods and manners of the days of Jesse Lee, and, as she said, "she did not fear the face of clay."

The last Sabbath evening that I attended church on the Cape, Uncle Eben led, in the absence of the regular minister.

All of the families in the town were represented in the meeting. It was a bad night, but there were present ten people each of whom had passed three-score and ten years. I was much impressed with the opening hymn, one of the primitive Methodist's : —

> "And let this feeble body fail,
> And let it faint and die."

Uncle read for a Scripture lesson, the Galilean parable of the rich fool, who provided everything for this life but deferred the interest of his soul. He illustrated the reading by a story, which seemed to impress the silent audience. It much impressed me. He said : —

"There was a young man that I once knew, who fell into evil habits, and was made constantly unhappy by his sense of wrong-doing and the fear of the consequences.

"Each evening when left alone, he reflected, and as often said, 'I will change my course of life to-morrow. I will to-morrow begin a life of obedience to God.'

"He would wait for the morning; but, when he arose and went out into the world, it was still to-day, so his old life went on.

"'I will not change my course to-day,' he said, 'I will fulfill my intention to-morrow. I have made to-morrow my reformation day.'

"Time went on, but it was always to-day. It was never the past; no day ever returned again, and to-morrow, the appointed day for his change of life, did not come.

"He fell sick. At the crisis of his disease he promised to begin a new life to-morrow. The next day he was better, but it was not to-morrow; it was still to-day.

"His mother was a God-fearing woman. When near death, she called him to her, and asked him for her sake to begin that life that has the promises of a better life than this.

"'I will do all that you ask. I have long been intending it.'

"'When will you begin?'

"'To-morrow.'

"But when to-morrow came, it was still to-day, and he did not fulfill his purpose.

"The frosts of years began to whiten his beard and hair. Age was stealing on. Each night as he looked into the glass, he saw the change, and he hurried to his slumbers with the thought, to-morrow I must begin the life that has the promises of heaven.

"Old age came at last. His wife died. Then his daughter died; a lovely girl. He promised each to begin a life of preparation for a future meeting. 'I will,' he said, 'begin to-morrow.'

"His life had reached four-score years, and yet it was always to-day. He fell sick, and the village pastor told him that he could not live.

"'How long shall I survive?' he asked.

"'The doctor says you may live until to-morrow.'

"'*That* is the day I have long waited for,' he said.

"In the night he asked:

"'What is the clock?'

"'Eleven.'

"Again he asked the same question.

"'Twelve.'

"Again.

"'One.'

"'It is still to-day, and there is no to-morrow.'

"He passed away in the morning, and the hours sped on, and for him there was no to-morrow, when rose or set the sun.

"Now, brothers and sisters, the time is yours. Speak as duty impels you."

"A number "testified." Then there was a pause.

"Improve the time, brothers and sisters," said Uncle, reprovingly.

Aunt Desire caught hold of the back of the seat in front of her and rose slowly. She took off her cotton gloves and dropped them on the seat and turned around, and faced the audience. She evidently had a burden on her heart, and had made up her mind to do her duty, and not to "fear the face of clay."

"My dear brothers and sisters, I feel just as I hadn't ought to, and when I feel just as I hadn't ought to myself, I feel like makin' good resolutions to do just as I ought to, and exhortin' other people to do as they ought to."

Uncle Eben evidently did not quite accept this logic. He turned the leaves of the Bible nervously, and raised his spectacles as though wondering what Desire would say next.

"My brothers and sisters, I'm going away for a spell to leave ye; I am goin' up to Jerusalem to attend the Feast of the Tabernacles."

She paused. One of the brethren said an encouraging "Amen," and presently she started off again in the direction of her first idea.

"And why don't ye do as ye ought to? When you read the *Zion's Herald*, and the *Journal*, and the *Transcript*, do you ever compare the lively doin' up to Boston with doin's down here by the cold streams of Babylon? Think of the Lecturship where they make clear to you all the mysteries of the world to come. Think of the faith that they exercise there, healin' all manner of diseases and takin' away the appetites of the vicious, and workin' all the miracles of the days of the prophets and apostles of old. I know that husband says that faith is not confined to places, and we can exercise it here as well as anywhere else; but he don't know everything, husband don't, no more than I do. But think of the good those peculiar people do. Societies—think of the societies—O you that live on the husks of the land down here by the cold streams of Babylon!—Societies for the Prevention of Cruelty to Animals, and Societies for the Prevention of Cruelty to Children, Women's

Dress Reform Societies, and here I've got three alpaca dresses more than I can wear, but I mean to reform, Prisoners Friend Societies, and societies for sendin' all wrong doin' people to the country; societies for the education of everybody, so that everybody can be educated, and societies to help everybody get rich, so that they may have money to give to the poor.  Think of the Missionary Societies, and the Mutual Aid Societies to make the widow's heart happy when her husband has gone, and the Art Societies and the Literary Societies; why, it seems as though all the people must be pious, and rich, and know near upon everything.

"Don't you see how far you come short of your duties and how you live below your privileges? It is true we haven't any drunkards to reform, and no prisoners to help.  I don't know as there are any paupers in the town, or any misbehavin' people.  But what of that?  You are not *miraculous*, like those Boston folks."

A brother near me groaned.

"Farewell, brothers and sisters, I am goin' up to Jerusalem to recuperate my faith.  I am goin' to see things with my own eyes.  I shall be with you in the spirit, and when I return I hope I shall have a tale to tell that will bring joy and gladness to all your hearts."

Aunt sat down. She looked relieved. So did uncle.

## CHAPTER XVI.

UP FROM THE CAPE. — A WALK. — AUNT CALLS ON THE DOCTORS.

I immediately returned home, and with feelings of great anxiety. I hurried from the Old Colony Depot across the city and Public Garden. Father himself answered my ring.

"I thought it was you," he said, cheerfully, laying his hand on my shoulder. "I think my letter must have frightened you; it was a false alarm. The doctor says there is no danger if I can only be kept quiet and get sleep. The difficulty is, I do not get any natural sleep. I am glad you have come. It will make me more quiet to have you here. Where is your aunt and Carrie?"

"They are coming in the carriage. I took the short cut from the depot. You cannot tell how relieved I am to find you better. Your letter *did* alarm me."

There was a worn, anxious look in father's face, and a strange light in his eyes. Something in his appearence made me uncertain about the doctor's sincerity. His cheerful appearance, however, reassured me, and the shadow passed away.

He had been accustomed to allude to Aunt Desire as "a character," and his invitations to Uncle and Aunt had never been very cordial or pressing: certainly not since the death of my own mother. My step-mother was an amiable woman, but a lover of society, and of her own circle of friends, and she took no interest at all in father's country relations. Eugene was her favorite stepson, and he seldom spoke with much respect of uncle and his family, whom he called "those people down on the Cape."

But when Aunt arrived from the depot, he met her at the door of the carriage, and the old friendship with "brother Eben's wife," was renewed after an almost silence of twenty years.

Few things in life ever gave me more pleasure than that meeting, and the interview in the parlor that evening. Father's mind on the latter occasion seemed to go back to the old farm; old associations, traditions and stories. He talked of the family burying-ground, the little church, and Pine Tree Hill.

"I was happy when I was a boy," said he;

"happier at night by the pasture's bars, than I have ever been since. Money cannot buy happiness, Desire. Health is happiness; hope is happiness; sleep is happiness. Did you ever realize, *sister*, what a blessing it is to be able to sleep?"

The word "sister" seemed to win Aunt's heart at once. Although she had said nothing to me, I knew that she had secretly some hard things in memory to overlook and forgive, in our family.

"No," said Aunt, "I never have thought about sleep at all. I just sleep. I should be sorry to be kept awake."

The evening passed pleasantly, but that night, after we had all retired to our chambers, there were mysterious sounds in father's room, as though he was walking, walking. At midnight, I was awakened by the same sound of incessant steps, and again near morning.

Father did not leave his room early in the morning. When he appeared, he assured Aunt and I that he was better, but there was a strange and mysterious expression as of great and resolutely controlled suffering in his face. I tried not to notice it.

Aunt had not seen him for years, and could not, like myself, mark the change by contrast.

We went out to walk in the morning — Aunt and I. The Public Garden was flaming with asters, and the air was full of the scent of the long, dark beds of heliotrope. The Beacon Street mall was an arch of leaves, tinted with autumn splendors. The white swan and the black swan were swimming in the pond, and Aunt was delighted with the scene as we passed from statue to statue.

Suddenly she asked, "Where is Boylston Street?"

"Right here," said I. "Why?"

"The doctors. You know that one reason why I have been wishin' to come up from the Cape is to see a reliable doctor."

"Dr. Warrenton lives *there*," said I. "Of excellent reputation. Experienced."

"Will you call with me?"

"Yes."

We found the doctor's rooms very antique and hung with pictures not very well calculated to make one hopeful and happy. There was a skull on an old clock which at once arrested Aunt's eye, and caused her to make the rather embarrassing remark that she "supposed that it once belonged to some poor critter or other some day or other." The table was full of medical periodicals, the contents of which were not over-cheerful and assuring. There was an open fire-place; the light was curtained, and Aunt grew nervous while waiting, as did I.

After a long time, a tall, lank, wrinkled-faced man appeared, like the foreman of a jury with the verdict.

"What can I do for you, Madam?"

"Dear me," said Aunt, "I've almost forgot. That skull up there's kind o' taken away my recollections. I've the catarrh. Is it dangerous?"

"I regard catarrh as consumption began." He looked squarely at Aunt like a statue.

"You don't, though."

"Let me look at your throat."

Aunt opened her mouth with the expression of a client waiting for the verdict.

"Congested. If that congestion was a little lower down you would not live two years," he added.

"How long have you had the catarrh?"

"Fifty years."

"Humph! and living yet."

"Jeff, let us go. I don't feel well. I always told Eben that I was not well. I been in consumption fifty years! Well, it is a blessin' that I did not know it."

"How much is to pay, doctor?"

"Five dollars for the examination,"

Aunt paid the tribute due to knowledge and experience.

"Jeff, I feel *awful.* I always thought I was consumptive. Let us consult the next doctor in the *row.*"

*He* was a middle-aged, quiet-looking gentleman. His apartment had a very *conservative* appearance.

Aunt stated her case in an anxious voice.

"The condition of which you speak," said he, "is not an uncommon one. In some cases it tends to serious disease; in others it prevents more serious disease: all depends upon the constitution. Whether it be a grave matter with you or not depends upon your constitution."

"Thank you," said Aunt, in a tone of relief; "how much is to pay?"

"Five dollars."

"I'm not quite so bad off as I thought I was. It all *depends,* you see. I hope it is not a *grave* matter with me, yet. Let us make one more call. Here, let us go in here, and hear what *he* says."

The next doctor was fat and jolly. His room

was full of landscape pictures, ornaments, vases of flowers.

"What is your disease, madame?"

"Consumption."

"How long have you had it?"

"Fifty years."

"Fifty years; let me examine your lungs. No, I need not do that. I never knew any one who had a pulse like yours to have any tendency to consumption."

"Well, I've got the catarrh!"

"Most people have in this climate; I look upon that disease as consumption prevented; acts as a sort of an issue; relieves the system. I've always noticed that catarrhal patients were very long lived, I wouldn't be surprised if you lived to be ninety, or more, and died of old age. When the tendency towards disease takes the form of catarrh, there's no telling how long a person may live."

"Jeff, I feel better. Don't I look better?"

"How much is to pay, Docter?"

"Oh, nothing; nothing ails you. Fine day; Public Garden looks splendid."

"Jeff, I am glad to be in the open air again. How beautiful the world looks! I like *that* doctor, don't you? How well I feel; come to think of it, the opinions of these two doctors are almost exactly like those of old Doctor Black and Doctor White down on the Cape. Strange, now isn't it?"

# CHAPTER XVII.

### DESIRE CALLS UPON SUNDRY EDITORS AND INTRODUCES TO THEM THE PASTORAL POEMS OF MISS FLORA PINK.

"Carrie, sit down a few moments, and let me tell you how I have been treated, here in Boston, too. I am disappointed in Boston editors. They are not the men I thought they were.

"Blanche Hale spent a few weeks at our house, some ten years ago, or more. She used to write for the magazines, and especially for the *Atlantic Monthly*. I asked her one day how she sent her contributions to the editor of the *Atlantic*. She said that her uncle, the Rev. Dr. Powers, took her first articles to Mr. Fields, and that Mr. Fields examined them, and accepted them, and invited her to call at the contributors' room.

"You should have heard her describe that contributors' room: Full of pictures, statues, and fine furniture, and free at all hours of the day to all who wrote for the magazine. When a person called with articles, he had only to send his card to Mr. Fields, who received him with bows and smiles, and paid him $200. A very 'gracious' man was Mr. Fields, so Blanche said; he had a generous and unselfish appreciation for everything good in a manuscript, and a helpful criticism for what was defective. That is the way Blanche expressed herself.

"Well, what Blanche said about the contributors' room and 'gracious' Mr. Fields, and about his 'generous and unselfish appreciation,' and 'helpful criticism,' impressed itself upon my mind like a picture. I thought if I took the poems of that poor, unfortunate girl, Flora Pink, to any editor's office, that I would be shown to the contributors' room, which would be full of pictures, statues, and fine furniture, and that some gracious man like Mr. Fields would come bowing in, read the poetry, and give me a check for $200. Flora needs the money so much, too.

"So I put a dozen or two of Flora's poems into my travellin'-bag, and made my way slowly in the direction of the Old South Church and Old State House, a way in which formerly all good people used to walk. I came to the office of a paper that I knew published poetry, and went in. There was a fine-looking old gentleman behind the counter.

"I walked up to him with an air of confidence.

"'Will you kindly tell me where the contributors' room is?' said I.

"'Compositors' room?' said he.

"'The room where they entertain ladies who bring valuable contributions to the paper,' said I.

"'Oh, the editor's room. Next door; up four flights.'

"I mounted the four flights of stairs; it was a long climb, but I do not mind hardships when I think I am carryin' happiness with me to another, much less when I am on a mission with the productions of genius for the consolation of the world.

"At the head of the fourth flight were the editors' rooms, marked *private*, but I walked right in, and findin' an empty chair, sat down, a little out of breath. A very fine-lookin' man was writin' at a quiet, sunny desk. He did not look up.

"'Hem, hem,' said I.

"But he did not turn his head.

"Then I proceeded to open my bag, and to take out Flora's poems, and look them over. I put those on 'Spring' in one parcel, and those on 'Autumn' in another; and those on 'Disappointed Hopes,' in another.

"'Hem! Hem!' says I.

"At that the intellectual lookin' man's pen seemed to fly faster than ever, and he looked as though all the world was outside of his own brain, and he wished it to remain so.

"'Are you the editor?' asked I.

"He looked up, very pleasantly.

"'How do you do, madam? I beg pardon, madam. I was very much engaged.'

"'Oh, I'm in no hurry,' said I, 'time isn't anything to me, just now, I'm visitin' in the city. Is this the contributors' room?'

"'We have no contributors' room,' said he. 'What do you wish, madam?'

"'I have here some poems that it will do your heart good to read. And a poorer girl than her who wrote them don't live down on the Cape. Here are ten poems on "spring" and ten on "autumn." I wish you would just read 'em and see what a genius that girl is; and so poor, too.'

"'But time is precious,' said he.

"'Oh, I'm in no hurry,' said I. 'I haven't anything in particular to do. I'm only visitin' in the city.'

"'But they are waiting for copy in the composing-room,' said he.

"'O, well, never mind, I can wait. I feel quite composed myself. Time is nothin' to me when I am visitin'.'

"'If you will leave one or two of your best contributions, madam,' said he, 'I will look them over as soon as I find time, and I will send you an answer by mail. Just put your address upon them.'

"'How would this do?' said I.

"I began to read an affecting ballad called the 'Two Orphans':

> "Two orphan children once there was,
> And why there was, was many a cause."

"'Kind of mysterious,' said I; 'like Emerson. "Once there was," that don't seem quite right.'

"A very distressed look came over his pleasant face. Then a boy came rushin' in, without any introduction.

"'The foreman wants the copy for the sixth page; all out of copy; waiting. Go to press an hour earlier this afternoon.'

"The boy flew out of the room.

"'Two orphan children once there was,'

read I. Guess I'll alter that, 'Once there *were.*' Have you a pencil?'

"'I am very busy, madam, this morning. Please leave your contribution on the desk.'

"'I'm in no hurry, but since it will be a convenience to you I'll leave it. Just send the money to that *there* place; I'm visitin' there. And remember that Flora is very poor. A poorer girl can't be found on the Cape. She needs just as much as you can pay. I'm sorry you are in a hurry this mornin'; I'm in no hurry. Just as well stay as not. Good-bye.'

"I left two poems. But after I got upon the stairs, I chanced to think that I had not made the correction, so I went back."

"'Will you allow me just to correct that grammar?' said I.

"'I will correct it if I accept the poem,' said the intellectual lookin' man.

"'Change "once there was," to "once there were?"'

"'Yes', said he, 'any way.'

"'Good by,' said I.

"'Good by.'

"When I got out on the stairs again, a thought came to me like a thunder clap. If that editor were to change 'once there was' to 'once there were' then the rhyme wouldn't come right.

'Why there was, was many a cause.'

"I turned round, and hurried back. The door of the editor's room stuck; I couldn't open it. I tried and tried, but it just *stuck*. So I came away.

"I went to the office of our religious paper. I found a lovely contributors' room there, carpeted, with pictures, book-cases and flowers. It was surrounded by little rooms where men were writin'. The rooms looked very pleasant, but the people all had occupied expressions on their faces, or a faraway appearance, such as some folks have when the contribution-box comes round.

"I went into one of the rooms.

"'Be you the editor?' asked I of a man readin' a paper that was printed only on one side.

"'I am one of the staff.'

"'I have brought you some poems on "Spring," written by Flora Pink. Flora is very poor. She —'

"'Excuse me, madame. This is a busy day. I am reading proof. If you will leave your articles, they will be given to the manuscript reader.'

"'Flora is very poor.'

"'Yes, madame, but we accept articles on their merits. It is our duty to give our readers the *best* material we can secure; the poverty of the author cannot influence us in this thing; that is a matter for charity, and our duties to the public and our duties to charity are distinct things. Do you see?'

"'The distinction is a fine one, as husband would say. But let me read you one of Flora's productions, and you will find that your duty to the public and to charity lie in the same direction.'

"I took out Flora's 'Apostrophe to Winter.' 'Apostrophe' seemed such an earthquake kind of a word that I knew it would command attention to what followed. It did. I began to read:—

'How cold is he, how icy cold,
As makes us shiver shakes untold.'

"'Here is another,' said I, 'entitled "The Battle Field Soldiers," suitable for the Fourth of July, or any patriotic day—

"We poor soldiers of the battle,
 Have to stand and hear the cannon rattle."

"Just then a voice was whistled right out of the wall, 'Is the proof ready?' 'I beg your pardon, madam,' said the gentleman. 'I must go to the Library at once. Leave your articles. They will receive attention soon after you are gone. Please leave a card with them.' So I left ten poems there with your card and came away.

"Next I went to the office of the *Youth's Instructor*. The editors' rooms are most unsociably high up there; it was like climbing to the top of Bunker Hill monument.

"I knocked. There was a dead silence. Then I knocked again. The door was opened by a youngish man with a very inquiring look in his face. He offered me a chair, and I opened my bag. He looked as though he was used to receiving contributors. There was a sort of polite, good-humored, easy despair about him, that must have been the result of long experience.

"I asked him if he was the editor. He said that he was one of the assistants, and acted for the editor when contributors called.

"I then told him Flora's story. He did not seem to be greatly affected, but heard me in a quiet, respectful way, as though he had heard of such cases before.

"'If you will write your address on the articles and leave them,' said he, 'they will receive attention at once. Here is a circular explaining our rules in regard to contributions.'

"'I will take the circular and read it.'"

"Here is a letter for you, Mrs. Endicott."

"A letter! I hope husband isn't sick or nothing. Why, why; its that —

'Two orphan children once there was.'

"Where's the check? No check, no note, no nothin'. Poor Flora."

"Here's a package a boy left for you, Mrs. Endicott."

"Why, why; it's that 'Shiver Shakes Untold' piece, and all the rest of them. How did it get here so soon? Got back almost as soon as I did. How wonderful! What Will Flora say?"

"Let me get that printed circular. How does it read?"

"Articles accepted are paid for. Those not accepted are returned to their authors, if *stamps* are sent or left with the manuscripts for the payment of postage. Declined manuscripts, not accompanied by post-office stamps, will not be returned."

"What does that mean?"

"Did you leave stamps?"

"No."

"Then it means that you will never hear from those poems again."

"But I'll call again."

"Will you — what does that say?"

"Articles should be sent by mail, and not left at the editorial office. The time of the editors cannot be given to personal interviews with writers, nor ought personal influence to be brought upon them by those seeking the acceptance of articles."

"Well, I never! It makes me hold my breath."

# CHAPTER XVIII.

### NOVEMBER.

Father did not improve. He grew weak in body, and seemed to lose mental control whenever he was excited. He could get little rest except under the influence of chloral; he was forming the chloral habit, and the daily reaction against the nightly drug was painful and pitiful to see.

My step-mother returned from Newport, and was greatly surprised and alarmed to find father so changed in appearance. Archie came back in time for the opening of the fall session of the schools, and we received a letter from Eugene, saying that he would return in November.

A peculiarity of father's condition was his intense likes and dislikes. He was governed wholly by his feelings, and yielded to his impulses without the exercise of reason. There were members of the family and several intimate friends whom he constantly shunned, and that without apparent reason. He liked to have aunt near him constantly, and her power to quiet him in his excitable moods was greater than any other's.

He made me his companion. He seemed to desire my constant attention; always liked to have me doing something that expressed my sympathy for him. If I were absent, he frequently inquired for me, and was restless until I returned.

We rode together on the beautiful October afternoons, in the bright suburbs of Brookline, among the villas of West Roxbury, over Milton Hill, by the Charles, among the Blue Hills, to the Newtons.

I gave nearly my whole time to him. If I proposed going anywhere by myself he would say, hopelessly : —

"Do not leave me, Jefferson, it will not be long."

These were sad days. They went on and on through the mid-autumn but brought no change. The trees of the Common turned to golden ashes, rustled and fell. The calm splendors of the October weather passed; the November winds came, and the Indian summer brought the last passing brightness of the year, but still no change.

Aunt wished to return to the Cape. Her suggestion of it made father worse, and the doctor urged her to stay until winter.

"Everything depends upon mental quiet," said the doctor. "He must not be crossed in anything. To oppose his will might prove suddenly fatal."

He wished Uncle Eben to visit him, and a letter was sent inviting and urging him to come. Uncle replied, promising to do so as soon as the fall work of the farm could be left to other hands.

He came in Indian summer. Father was immediately better on meeting Uncle; his spirits revived; the two talked of old days and their early associations, and father seemed to live again in the years long passed. The doctor spoke hopefully. The cloud seemed passing. How I longed for the old home calm again — after the fever.

Aunt and I went out much together, now that uncle had come. We were cheerful again, for the doctor said that father would soon be better. In our lives was an Indian summer weather.

Aunt one day made the call that she had promised herself on the Cape, on Richard Follett — Hon. Richard Follett — Dick Follett of the Cape.

He had been a poor boy, but by great, persistent Yankee shrewdness and energy, had become rich. He was one of the many farmers' boys of the Cape, who had brought to a city experience, the force of right early training, good health, a clear mind and an active ambition, and had prospered. After his first business successes he had made it his untiring purpose of life to acquire wealth. His aims turned into gold.

His house in the suburbs was imposing — a colonial mansion in a broad lawn, surrounded by fine specimens of landscape gardening, and grand old trees. It showed that his love of country life had not changed. The estate was like a park in the thickly-peopled streets.

We rode into the grounds. Though late in the season, a fountain was playing, and the carefully guarded flower-beds were still in bloom.

A group of polite children followed the servant to meet us at the carriage, expecting to welcome some well-known friend.

We were cordially received by Mrs. Follett, who had heard her husband speak of Aunt, and she introduced her cheerfully to her children. She was a very gracious lady; one of those whose spirit is the light of home.

But when Aunt asked to see "Richard," her face and manner changed. She looked troubled, and was for a few minutes silent.

"Have you not heard? said she.

"Husband has not been well of late. Incessant care, those business cares that leave one no time for recreation, you must understand, Mrs. Endicott, broke down his nervous system, and for the last two years he has not been able to enjoy the results of his business efforts. It is very sad. I would be glad to have you meet him, Mrs. Endicott, but it would not be well. He seldom sees his own children. His case is a very peculiar one. He is very low-spirited; a very peculiar case. I do not always feel quite free to speak of it. I only do so to his old friends."

"He is surrounded with everything to make one happy," said Aunt. "He has wealth and honors, a beautiful home and lovely children. I am sorry that he cannot enjoy life. What form does his melancholy take?"

"We seldom speak of it," she reiterated hesitatingly, "you will think it very strange, but he constantly imagines that we are poor and shall *come to want.*"

We rode away from the grand old estate of the over-worked man.

Aunt remarked thoughtfully on the way home:—

"Eben has right views about some things, hasn't

he, Jefferson? Ambition is a good thing, but it is something to be contented, and to do one's daily duties as they come to you, and to live for the longer life that follows this. Taxed for a million, yet thinks he is comin' to want. Does not have the society of his own children. Poor Richard: there are men who are richer in happiness in their cottages on the Cape.

"The fact is, Jefferson," she added, "it takes a great deal of livin' and experience to understand life. We read the book backwards, many of us do. It is well to take time in life to stop and think."

I think Aunt is right. It takes much experience to understand life, and too many read the book backwards.

# CHAPTER XIX.

### EUGENE RETURNS FROM ETRETAT.

Eugene has returned from Etretat. He is not pleased to find Uncle and Aunt here, and has gone to stay at the Club until those "wulgar, wagabondish people," as he expresses it, "go" back to the Cape. Father did not meet Eugene very cordially, and I am sure Uncle and Aunt do not quite like him, although I heard Aunt say:

"Eben, just see what your boys might have been!"

Eben shook his head in silence. He evidently would not have been pleased to have had one of his "boys" return home dressed like Eugene and seemingly only ambitious to imitate the habits of the sons of decaying families he had met abroad.

Eugene has "lost his interest in America." So he says. He is interested chiefly in English Tory politics, and regrets the fall of Beaconsfield. He has become a Ritualist, and regards the "Oxford movement" as "the beginning of a holy pilgrimage back to Rome."

He condemns our free school system. He has received new light on many social problems.

"The education of the children of the poor is all a meestake," he said yesterday, in Uncle's hearing. "It makes them discontented. It gives them an ambition to rise above the callings in which — aw — they are most useful. One has to live abroad in order to see how great a meestake it is."

Uncle colored. The toe of his boot moved back and forth under the easy chair like a shuttle. He did not reply.

Eugene has become an admirer of the new school of art. He condemns melody in music, and color in painting. "Melody and color," he says, "are the delights of the wulgar."

"I always thought," said Uncle, "that the prose of music was merely used to heighten the effect of the poetry, or melody — and that melody was the true music of the sentiments. So in painting, as in nature. I have supposed that low tones, mutual tints, shades, were contrasts to heighten the effect of color. I fail to see why in art the lower should be made to take the place of the higher, or the less put for the greater."

"It is not possible to discuss art except with

people who are trained to art, and belong to its inner circles. Reason has nothing to do with the matter at all. Reason is for the multitude; art is for the few. The common mind cannot understand. This is why so few comprehend the religion of art: I mean symbols. All outward religion is a majestic symbolism." He added: —

"We need in this country great masters to build grand temples like those of the old world, and fill them with symbols by which truth is prefigured. Then we shall not be ashamed of our name. Boston would be, indeed, St. Botolph's, and New York worthy of the duke whose name she bears."

"You may be right," said Uncle Eben, in a restrained tone. "But I do not so read history In the Rome of art the Coliseum grew and crimsoned with human blood; in the Athens of art the strength of Greece wasted and decayed. Israel, under the judges, was stronger than amid the splendors of the reign of Solomon; and the Rome of the Republic, than the Rome of the emperors in all their gold and purple. Art does not change character. It is another power which does that. As a servant of good, art is noble; of evil, despicable. Art, as art, is nothing at all."

Eugene touched upon politics.

"What we need," he says, " is a grand constitutional monarchy, with titled families trained to government, under whose gracious influence the higher arts would flourish, and the æsthetic aspects of religion grace our cities and glorify our national name."

"I don't think I agree with him," said Aunt, in an undertone, "but it is fine to hear a young man talk like that. It shows that he is an original thinker, and has spirit. I wish our boys could have had some of the advantages of modern culture — not have just gone out West to fight the 'border ruffians,' in old Jim Buchanan's days."

"The renascent days are coming," continued Eugene. He twirled his moustache, twirled his cane, and walked into the hall.

"The renascent days do seem to be on their way," said Uncle to me. "After Cromwell came Charles II. When young men cease to vote; when the church bestows more thought on what pleases the eye and the ear, than upon inward life; when faith in good declines, and saloons multiply; when art is put for virtue, the renascent days will come, and a period like that of the Merry Monarch will follow the age of the Hamptons and Miltons."

Uncle looked troubled. I could see that he had taken a positive dislike to Eugene, and that each had a sort of inward contempt for the opinions of the other.

Eugene came ambling in from the hall.

"Etretat was such a swell place. There was at one time the families of a dozen noblemen there, and the young men were such swells! There is nothing on earth that I so much admire as fine young English gentlemen."

"Except of course, a fine young American gentleman," said uncle. "Of the old school, I mean. Such as you often meet at your club, do you not? A young man with the principles and bearing of Sir Henry Vane?"

"So you seem to think that the young American gentleman of the old school made a finer figure in society, than *we* of to-day?"

"He was certainly stronger in politics, in the church, and in manly independence of character. He was not less cultivated or courteous. For example, let me illustrate:" —

I felt that uncle was about to give Eugene a democratic lesson that would be clear, and that it would somehow have reference to the Duke of York.

He continued :—

"The somewhat recent Penn celebration in Philadelphia, brought distinctly into view the character of the founder of Pennsylvania. It was the character of William Penn that schooled the Province, and that has made the history of Pennsylvania exceptionally noble and honorable. Penn's hand sowed the seed that blossoms in the prosperous towns and communities on the banks of the Schuylkill and the Susquehanna, in the great industries of Harrisburg and Pittsburg, and in the conscientiously used wealth and culture of Philadelphia.

"He had been shocked at Christ College at the irreligion and immorality that everywhere prevailed. The gay court of Charles was poisoning all the higher circles of society, and especially the literary institutions. The Church bowed obsequiously before statesmen of most corrupt character. An age of wit, license, insincere politeness, and enervating pleasures followed the stern rule of Cromwell : the age of the Cavaliers.

"There were not wanting strong-minded men, who protested against these tendencies to moral decay. Among them were the Quakers. A few students at Christ Church College were among the protestants, and foremost among these students was the handsome youth, William Penn.

"He cloistered his serene intellect amid the gayeties around him, and studied the lives of good men, and stored his memory with the golden thoughts of good books. He found his conscience at war with the brilliant court that his father, Admiral Penn, delighted to honor. He felt that an age of darkness had come, and the young commoner began to dream of a Christian democracy, founded on right principles, that should practice the virtues of self government in a new land. Out of this dream came the province and state of Pennsylvania.

"He heard of the Quakers, and met Thomas Loe, an obscure disciple of George Fox. Under the influence of this man, young Penn made the resolution *not* to conform to the usages of the gay society of the time.

"His father heard of his non-conformity with pain. The old Admiral was a most prosperous man. He was Naval Commissioner, Admiral of Ireland, a member of Parliament, and a favorite of the Duke of York. He spread a jovial table, and entertained the best company.

"He resolved to bring his son to London and to see "what hard dining and late dancing" would do in weakening and destroying his new principles. He took him to the theatres, gave him a dog and gun, ridiculed him and had him whipped, and finally sent him to Paris, with introductions to the gay society of the French capital.

"Young Penn was somewhat influenced by these dramatic episodes of life, but his principles were not changed.

"When about twenty three years of age, he went to Cork, sick of the garish scenes and false lights that had so long glittered before him. Soon after his arrival he learned that Thomas Loe, the Quaker, was about to preach in that city. He resolved to hear him.

"The plain Quaker, the apostle of the Inner Light, announced the subject of his discourse.

"It was: 'There is a faith that overcomes the world and there is a faith that is overcome by the world.'

"Penn was smitten by the subject. He felt that it was a message to him. That night he turned his back forever upon an idle and purposeless life, andbecame a Friend.

"Hat homage was the custom of the age.

"'Friends do not take off their hats to any man,' said Penn to his father, when they again met.

"'How will you do at Court, you will not wear your hat in the presence of the Prince?'

"'Let me have a little time to consider the question.'

"He retired to his room, and prayed.

"He returned saying in effect that he would not render pretentious homage to any man.

"'Not even to the King and the Duke of York?'

"'No, not even to the King and the Duke of York.'

"His father demanded that he should leave his house.

"He did so, but he had within him that which is of more consequence than titles and estates, 'the faith that overcomes the world.'

"That type of young men is disappearing in the East, but reappearing somewhat less heroically in the West. The Winthrops of the first century, the Adamses of the second, the Wendell Philippses of this; their simple habits, principles, and strong purposes, are not the types and models of the new order of things. Young men are putting on the old clothes of the Middle Ages, and one sees second-hand Europe everywhere. The independence of thought and character that ennobles a man for all time, seems to have passed away with the war. Yet, a crisis like the war would bring it back again. I believe in our people still."

Eugene was an intense admirer of what is distinctively English, and of old English scenes and associations.

"When I was in England," he said one October morning, when he had called to ask about father, "when I was in England, I visited as many of the places associated with Dickens' books as I was able to find: Falstaff Inn, Goswell Road, Rochester Castle, White Hart Inn, Gray's Inn, Ralph Nickleby's Mansion, Old Bailey Prison, Old Curiosity Shop, Chancery Lane, Lincoln Inn, Blue Bell Inn, Epping Forest. I spent many days in these places, book in hand. It was charming, charming!"

"That reminds me," said uncle. "I would like to visit some of the places associated with old-time Boston. I wish you would go with me this morning, Eugene, you are so fond of historic places."

"What places are they, uncle?"

"Well, first to the place where Mary Chilson is buried."

"Mary Chilson? — Mary Chilson? I think I have not heard much about Mary Chilson? Who was she?"

"She was the first to leap upon Plymouth Rock."

"Oh — aw — *where from?*"

"From the boat of the Mayflower."

"Oh — aw — I beg your pardon. I really, weally don't know where *that* place is."

"Let us go and see the Boston Stone."

"The Boston stone? I beg your pardon. I really, weally never heard of the Boston Stone — the Boston Stone? How curious. I beg your pardon."

"Well, then, let us go and see the remains of the old Province House."

"I have read of the old Province House in Twice Told Tales — charming, all very charming; it was, I think, near the Old South Church. I did not know that there were any remains. You have the advantage of me, you see. I beg your pardon."

"Then we will go to see the Old Codfish at the State House."

"I do know where the State House is, Uncle. That is a very *evident* building. But Uncle, I beg your pardon, I wouldn't like to go to see an old *codfish*, Uncle, really, weally I wouldn't."

## CHAPTER XX.

AUNT RELATES TO UNCLE HER LUMINOUS CONVERSATION WITH MR. MCBRIDE, THE AGNOSTIC.

"Husband, have you ever met Mr. McBride? He is a handsome gentleman, with a sprinklin' of gray in his hair; round as a Dutchman, with rosy cheeks, very social, and always ready to converse on any subject. I asked Carrie one day to what religious denomination he belonged, and she said he was an Agnostic. I did not know just what that meant, but supposed that it was one of the high sects, and that he must have some mysterious sources of knowledge, as edifyin' as the Lectureship, and as I wished to get as much light as possible, I thought I would have an interview with Mr. McBride whenever I should have a good opportunity.

"There was one thing about Mr. McBride that puzzled me: He was rich, he had been educated at college, he had travelled in foreign countries, he went into the best society; as Carrie described him, 'he was a club-house bachelor,' with every advantage that the world can give, and yet he was not contented or happy. He seemed runnin' after happiness all the time but never findin' it. He was not a hopeful man; he did not believe in people. With all of his wealth and learnin' there seemed to be something wantin', notwithstandin' that he was an Agnostic.

"One evenin' he called when Henry's wife was out, and Henry was quiet, and I found myself left alone with him. Now, thought I, is my opportunity; now I will plunge into the deep sea of knowledge and experience, and 'bring up pearls,' to use a figure.

"'Mr. McBride,' said I, 'would you have any objection explainin' to me your theological views? You belong to one of the high sects, I hear.'

"'My theological views?—Don't you know, my dear madam, I'm an Agnostic,' said he.

"'Have you any objection, Mr. McBride to tellin' me your experience?' said I. 'We meet around to the houses and tell our experiences on the Cape, and we find it wonderful edifyin'.'

"'No, madam;' said he 'no objection. It is a sad story. I sought for the truth everywhere, with this result, to become an Agnostic. I studied theology; I read science; I argued with ministers of all creeds. I used to love to argue, and I have spent hours and hours in the studies of the first and best ministers in Boston, but I was brought to no conviction of the truth. I resolved to go abroad and study the German systems of philosophy. I spent two years in Berlin, but found no satisfaction. Many were the hours that I passed in the summer beer gardens, with students of theology and science, as curious as myself, but I was not able to arrive at any definite conclusion. I left the land of the Reformation, and went to Paris. Oh, the hours that I have spent in the Boulevards, smoking my cigars and discussing the mysteries of the soul! I studied Hegel, and Strauss and Compte. I became a Pessimist. Then I went to England and pursued my inquiries in the great club houses, where the wits and philosophers meet. I made myself more familiar with the theories of Darwin, Tyndall and Spencer. But the truth was not to be found anywhere. My travels and studies were all in vain. I have discussed this matter of theology with ministers of all churches, with philosophers of all schools, with scientists, artists and poets. I have sought and found nothing.'

"'But I thought you were an Agnostic?' said I.

"'So I am, madam,' said he.

"'What is an Agnostic?' asked I.

"'It is a man that don't pretend to know anything,' said he.

"'And you don't pretend to know anything?' said I.

"'No.'

"'Well, I might have knowed as much — you don't seem like a man who had any spare knowledge to sell, or to give away. But Carrie said how that you was an Agnostic, and I thought my first impressions must be wrong. Mr. McBride, I hope you will excuse me, I am a very plain spoken woman,' said I, 'but I always do my duty, and I do not fear the face of clay.'

"'Mr. McBride, I would like to ask you a few philosophical questions,' said I.

"'Proceed, madam. I shall be pleased to endeavor to answer them.'

"'If you were going a fishing, you wouldn't go up to the top of a granite mountain, now, would you?'

"'Certainly not, madam.'

"'Nor go out into the middle of the sea to look for fruits, or flowers?'

" 'No, madam.'

" 'You wouldn't split open a rock if you were looking for your eye-glass?'

" 'I certainly should not, madam. But what have your questions to do with this great problem?'

" 'I'm coming to that,' said I. 'You say you have searched the land and sea, and studied all the philosophies, to find the truth, and you can't?'

" 'Yes, madam.'

" 'Well, hundreds of people on the Cape have found the truth who never went twenty miles from home, and never studied the philosophies, or saw Paris. I know of one man who found the truth, and never so much as left his bed.'

" 'Extraordinary! Where?' he asked.

" 'Where? In the only place that it is to be found — in his soul.'

" 'I see you are a mystic,' said he.

" 'No, there's nothin' mysterious about it at all. I'll tell ye how, you needn't have gone roamin' all over the world; if you had just come to me, I could have made the thing clear; I understand it perfectly; the truth isn't lost. You just give up all these selfish habits of yours, and wrong desires, and open your heart to the truth, and the truth will come to you naturally. Open the curtains of your soul to the light, and the light will come in.'

"'Very poetic, madam,' said he.

"'If I were in your case, I'll just tell you what I would do: I would throw away my cigars, and leave off drinkin' beer, and let the club-houses all go, and I would repent of my sins,—and you look as though they might be quite numerous, and—

"'Goin'?' asked I.

"'Good night, madam,' said he.

"'Poor Mr. McBride, I'm afraid he'll never find the truth. And so an Agnostic is one that knows nothin' at all. Why, Eben, we needn't have taken so much pains to study up these deep things — I knew more than that myself, when I was down on the Cape. *He* didn't pretend to know nothin' at all, and he called himself by that great high-soundin' name, and didn't seem ashamed of it."

# CHAPTER XXI.

## "UP AND DOWN THE HARBOR GOES THE HENRY MORRISON!" — UNCLE'S NARRATIVE.

"Up and down, up and down the harbor goes the *Henry Morrison.* Every day but Sunday, with its cells and its young passengers, on, on, through the years!

"My heart turns sick to think of it; it brings tears to my eyes, and yet the officer said to me:

"'That is nothing, not a drop in the bucket; these things are but the incidents and accidents of crime.'

"'Incidents and accidents!' and yet so many criminals and so young!"

Uncle walked to and fro, and I asked him to what he referred.

"I have to-day visited Deer Island; I wished to see the institutions, and they gave me a 'pass' at City Hall.

"While I was standing upon the deck, waiting for the boat to start, and looking at the floating ice on the harbor, as it glistened in the noon-day sun, several policemen and quite a number of hard-looking lads gathered upon the wharf, as if expecting an arrival. Presently several close, padlocked carriages, marked 'City of Boston,' were driven down to the pier.

"I walked forward to see who the new comers were."

"'Stand back, gentlemen,' said an officer, 'stand back till we get these prisoners on board, so that we may see who they are, and not get the crowd mixed.'

"This seemed a doubtful compliment to the 'gentlemen,' and as we had no wish to get 'mixed up' with the people whom the officers were assisting out of the carriages, we stepped back, leaving so broad a dividing line as to preclude the possibility of any mistake.

"The scene was a sad one. Nearly seventy prisoners, most of them young, and nearly half of them girls and young women, were brought on board of the boat. Monday, and most of these prisoners had been arrested for drunkenness or disorderly conduct on the Sabbath!

"The prisoners were a motley company. Several of the boys seemed to be Americans, and the young men, for the most part, foreigners. They were all sober, now, and their conduct was such as befitted their humiliating situation.

"As they stepped from the vehicles, and became conscious that the people on the wharf and the boat were looking at them, they hung their heads, and with averted looks and downcast eyes, were conducted below deck.

"'Good-by, Harry,' said a middle-aged woman, as one of the boys passed her on the wharf.

"The tears were rolling down her cheeks, and the head of the boy dropped lower.

"'Good-by, mother.'

"The boy did not look up. He was ashamed to meet the face of his own mother.

"The behavior of the girls was wholly different from that of the boys and men. Girls less seldom lose their self-respect than boys, but it is said that when they do fall into evil ways they are far more brazen and reckless.

"The female prisoners came on board laughing, or giving themselves airs, as though the whole thing were a joke, or they were wholly indifferent to public opinion. Not even the youngest of them seemed at all affected by the disgrace of her situation, and not one of them shed a tear.

"I was informed that many of these girls had before been sentenced to the Island, and that one of them, in particular, had been committed to the Reform School twenty-nine times, and to the House of Industry a number of times.

"After the prisoners came on board, the boat left the wharf for the Island. By my side sat an old lady who was going to the alms-house. She was neatly dressed, her face bore the lines of disappointment and sorrow, and she was bitterly weeping. Of course she alone knew what caused the tears to flow, but they evidently were associated with her dismal prospects in life and her hard lot. Occasionally some particular thought seemed to be more painful than the others, and her tears broke out afresh as often as it came to her mind. She looked like one who had struggled against poverty and the alms-house, but was now prostrated, broken and hopeless.

"'Have you any children?' asked an officer.

"'Yes, but they are all scattered. I don't know where they are. I used to live with Noel, my youngest boy, and he was good to his mother till he took to bad ways.'

"At these words her grief broke out anew. She buried her face in her bundle, and tried to suppress an audible burst of anguish. And in this way the poor, friendless, deserted mother, robbed by vice even of her youngest boy, always a mother's darling, continued her broken-hearted way to the home of the friendless.

"It was a hard case, but shall I ever forget the young woman that sat by her side, a stranger, hating God and the world. How she did run on! I seem to hear her now.

"'Hypocy," said the officer, 'rescued her from suicide — trying to drown herself under the bridge.'

"'Life,' she said, 'I hate it. I was happy once, and decent, and had a home and a child. God knows how I loved that husband and child. Then *he* took to drink. The saloon-keepers tempted him. He grew worse — but I loved him, and when I went to the saloon-keeper and begged him for the sake of my child to save *him*, he jeered at me. Then he went to the bad, and the city that had put temptation before him, put him behind the bars. Then my child took sick and became a cripple, and *I* took to bad ways. I had not a friend in the world.

"'I went down under the bridge, last night, for the waters to rise and cover me. *The tide was out.*'

I thought of my old mother, long ago dead. Blessed are the dead. *The tide began to come in.* It cooled my feet. I thought of my old home, and the trees, and the martins under the eaves, and morning-glories. *The tide was coming in.* I thought of the old school-house, the old church, and the choir in which I used to sing. *The tide was rising.* I thought of my early love for William. How happy I was — how I trembled with delight when he first told me that he loved me! *The tide was rising.* I thought of my happiness when I first kissed my baby. Then I thought of woe — Oh, God, how I suffered! *The tide was rising.*

"'Then *he* came and dragged me out, and pulled me in my wet clothes through the street, and past *that* saloon, and that saloon-keeper put out his head and jeered at me.

"'It is *he* who ought to be here, not I. This city licenses men to destroy family and hearts and happiness, and the officials fatten on the wages of death. It bids men destroy men, and sends the wives of those that men destroy to the Island. It protects the lights of hell that glimmer in every street. It says "Allure, destroy!"

"'Go away, stranger; don't preach. I hate you!

I hate everybody. I cannot help myself. I wish I were dead.'

"How wildly she glared at me! How she changed her voice at the words 'the tide was rising.' How many saloons does the city license? How many men to rob and murder their brothers, and mock at their families?

"As I turned from her she added: —

"'Stranger, you look kind, as though you came from the country, and had not been hardened by such sights as these. My little boy — how I loved him when he was a baby, poor thing, before I took to the bad — sells papers on Columbus Avenue, perhaps you would be willing to do something for him; if you should, God bless you; he is a cripple.'"

"When we arrived at the Island, the prisoners were taken to the Reception-House, a brick building near the wharf. I was invited into the officer's apartment, where I remained during the calling of the roll of the prisoners.

"'Richard Honar.'

"'Here.'

"'How old are you?'

"'Twenty.'

"'Where were you born?'

"'In Ireland.'

"'Can you read and write?'

"'No.'

"'Have you a trade?'

"'No.'

"'Have you been here before?'

"'Yes.'

"'Under what name?'

"'James Scott.'

"The officers informed me that many of the prisoners came to the Island under assumed names, and that some of them had changed these names so many times as to have almost forgotten what their real names were.

"The same questions were put to each of the prisoners. The men and boys answered with an evident sense of humiliation, but the girls exhibited the same brazen effrontery as when on the wharf.

"'Mary Alton.'

"'Here!' with a toss of the head, a pout of the lips, and a forced smile on meeting the eye of a companion.

"'How old are you?'

"'Eighteen.'

"'Have you ever been here before?'

"'O yes,' with a laugh.

"'Under what name?'

"'Mary Dennis.'

"One of the boys was quite young. He gave his name as Johnny. He looked neglected, and his face showed a certain refinement of feeling and a good heart.

"I said to him, 'Johnny, how came *you* here?'

"'No cause, sir; I'm a vagrant.'

"'Have you any friends?'

"'Only an aunt.'

"'Were you ever here before?'

"He seemed ashamed to answer, colored deeply and said, —

"'Not while mother and sister were living.'

"The prisoners were formed into a line, and were conducted along the icy road to the institution, a part of them having been sentenced to the House of Reformation, and a part to the House of Industry.

"'These are not our criminals,' said the officer.

"'*They* go to other places.'

"Up and down, up and down the harbor goes the *Henry Morrison*. With its cells. With its young passengers.

"Up and down, up and down, daily.

"I pity them from my heart. I have no hard words; I can but recall Robert Hall's expression on seeing a poor drunkard dragging himself along the streets of London — 'But for the grace of God, there goes Robert Hall.'

"I never dreamed this fair city had such a side as this. Few country people do. Up and down, up and down the harbor — Heaven pity them!

"Degraded? Yes, in life, but hardly more so in heart than the man whose vote protects the ghouls that feed and fatten on the souls of men!

## CHAPTER XXII.

#### INTELLIGENCE FROM TREASURE MOUNTAIN.

"Are we alone, Jefferson? Something has happened. I have a secret on my mind, and I have been waitin' for a chance to speak to you about it, all by ourselves.

"I wouldn't have husband know of it for anything; when I speak of that affair his mouth begins to pucker — you know what husband is — and such a wife as I have been to him, too!

" *What affair*, do you ask?

" Why, Treasure Mountain.

" It isn't best to trust in riches, Jefferson. They take to themselves wings, and where they fly or go to no man knows.

"I have been to Dr. Gamm's office, privately, for a settlement, four times, and yesterday, and yesterday, I was stunned, I was *stunned* at the word that was left me. I came home that astonished that I never saw a person or a house on any of the streets; that astonished I was — and I hesitate to tell it, even to you.

"The first time I went, I asked for the Doctor, and was told to send my card into the inner office. I told the boy that I hadn't any card, but to tell the Doctor that Desire Endicott wanted to see him, she that he boarded with down on the Cape.

"The boy returned.

"'The Doctor is very busy with important business. He says you will have to call some other day,' says he.

"Now I boarded that man and his wife for $5 a week, for six weeks, both of 'um. And they lived high. Then I let him have $500 to pull down Treasure Mountain, so as to found the University, and do good. Should you have thought that he would have sent me such a message as that ; should you have thought it ?

"I called the next day and received almost exactly the same answer; would you have thought it ?

"I was determined not to be put off the third time. So I wrote him a note. It was as follows, very polite and respectful : —

"'Mrs. Endicott presents her compliments, and wishes to draw her dividens on Treasure Mountain. She would like principal and interest. She will wait until you can give her an interview. This is her third visit.

Desire Endicott.'

"I sent this into the inner office by the boy. After a long time the boy brought me back a slip of paper. It read like this: —

"'An explanation of this affair will be left for you to-morrow with the clerk at the desk. I am very busy to-day. M. O. Gamm.'

"I thought this was rather indefinite. But business is business, and busy men, I said to myself, cannot let light matters like $500 stand in the way of great transactions. *He told* me that Company had a capital of $10,000,000. So I overlooked the way he treated me, or I tried to, and the next day went with my big wallet in my inner skirt pocket, so that no thieves would get at it, to draw principal and interest, and end my connection with the great enterprise.

"I asked the clerk for the Doctor.

"'He has gone,' said he.

"'Where?' asked I.

"'To Chicago.'

"'Did he leave my money?' said I.

"'He left no money for any one.'

"'No word?'

"'Nothing.'

"'Yes, he did,' said that little errand-boy; 'he told me, just as he was leaving, to tell you that if that old woman from Cape Cod called, just to say that there Treasure Mountain affair all *busted up* long ago, and to give her one of them printed reports.'

"Could I believe my own ears! Well, I brought away the printed report. It isn't interestin' readin'! I wish I had listened to what husband said. But I am pretty firm-minded, and I am not goin' to tell Eben anything about it, now, would you? He'd just say, 'I told you so.' And such a wife as I have been to him, too! I never wanted to scold so in my life, but who is there to scold at?

"Eben just offered me $100 to spend; he's a good provider. I didn't accept it; I hold my head high in times like these. I expected to have had my dividens from Treasure Mountain for spendin' money and for charity. Why, I'd better have let my money been in the Savin's Bank down on the Cape; now hadn't I?

"'That old woman from Cape Cod!' after all I had done for him, too. 'All busted up!'

"THAT IS ALL BUSTED UP."

There's my big wallet, the thieves may have it for all me; flat as a flapjack. I have often seen that wallet, in the visions of the night, as I expected it would look when I came to a settlement with Treasure Mountain. It never looked like that.

"I haven't shown my *capabilities* after all. A woman wa'n't made to speculate, now, was she? But I have done as well as some of the men. I've got my report.

"Jefferson, one can never tell what a day may *not* bring forth."

# CHAPTER XXIII.

THE BLACK SEA. — UNCLE EBEN'S NARRATIVE, CONTINUED.

"The story told me by the wretched creature on the *Henry Morrison* has haunted me. As a change from the sick room I several times walked over to Columbus Avenue, hoping to meet her little son, the newsboy.

"I found him — it was as she had said — he was a thin shadow of life — he flitted into and out of the cars, on his crutch, like a ghost.

"I could not overcome the feeling in my heart that I had a mission to do, and used to go down and buy a portion of his little stock of papers, not caring to be particular about the change. I cannot forget the look of gratitude that he used to give me as he stood in the gaslight, and how he seemed to drink in the words that indicated that I cared for him — like a soul thirsting for sympathy and affection, and conscious of being unloved.

"One day I missed him. The other newsboys

of whom I made inquiry concerning him said he was sick.

"The days passed on until one Saturday evening a little boy touched my arm in the street, and said : —

"'Freddy is dead. May I sell you papers now?'

"'When did Freddy die?'

"'This morning.'

"'Had he anyone to take care of him?'

"'He lived with an old woman.'

"'Where?'

"'At ——, North Street.'

"North Street — I went to the place.

"The stranger who visits Boston, and sees its beautiful churches and fine public buildings, its green Common, surrounded with elegant homes, its Public Garden, with statues, fountains, and flowers, and the evidences of wealth, refinement and culture that meet him on every hand, can have little conception of such a place as North Street.

"I found it a locality filled with tippling shops and dens of vice; with hard, miserable men, from whom all that is godlike in human nature seemed to have departed, and yet more miserable women, who shrink from the very face of day.

"I found the place where he lived, and inquired of the house-keeper —

"'When is Freddy's funeral?'

"'I don't know; Mr. —— comes after him to-morrow.'

"'Who is Mr. ——?'

"'He buries folks for the city.'

"I sought the city undertaker.

"'Do you bury a newsboy from North Street to-morrow?'

"'Yes.'

"'Where?'

"'At Mount Hope. Did you know him? Perhaps you would like to go to the cemetery with me to-morrow?'

"'I would.'

"'And,' then he added, as we separated, 'probably you will be the only mourner at the newsboy's funeral.'

"It was a Sabbath afternoon, calm, still, golden. I kept my appointment, and, as Mr. —— predicted, I was the only mourner, or at least the only friend who followed the little wanderer to his last resting place. As I mounted the seat with the driver, I saw in the back of the vehicle a little pine coffin, and I was made doubly sad by the thought that it was one for which no man cared.

"We passed down the pleasant streets, overarched with bright leaves. The churches seemed flowing and reflowing with the long tide of people. The Common, with its hazy, dreamy avenues, presented a scene of life, beauty and contentment, covered as it was with light, happy faces. Harrison Avenue stretched before us like a winding stream of sunlight, over which flitted the shadows of long lines of trees, and sweetly sounded the mellow notes of the church bells — then away through streets where untold rural beauties mingled with the embellishments of art, and every thing, heightened in the loveliness by the Sabbath calm, made the blooming earth appear like the very borders of a better land.

"'All Paradise seemed mirrored in the trees;
The same God made both heavenly flowers and these.'

"Forest Hills! What a vision of loveliness on any day! How beautiful on the Sabbath! The great city lay behind us at last, and we passed before a great gate, over which was written, 'I AM THE RESURRECTION AND THE LIFE.'

"We soon were at Mount Hope — at the Potter's Field.

"They had dug his grave in God's acre, removed from the places of monuments and statues — in a quiet spot where the slumberers are sooner forgotten—though only a little sooner, after all—than those who sleep under the costly sculpture and the tall shaft.

"An Irishman was waiting for us, leaning on his spade over the little heap of earth on one side of the grave. Then we took out of the carriage the little coffin, and set it down on the green earth.

"'Twas the last time. Only one remove more was to be made, and the lame newsboy would be laid away forever from the green leaves and the sunshine, from the flowers and the singing of the birds.

"The silent sunshine fell upon his coffin, and slanted into his little grave. Where was his mother on this sad day? *Who* was she? Where did she come from?

"They took up the coffin and laid it down again, this time under the sod. They shovelled the earth in quickly, and left the mound to the wild flowers.

"Fatherless, motherless, sisterless, friendless! My heart condemned me as I turned from the little grave, because I had not been of still greater service to the young life so quickly ended, but I thanked God that He had led me to speak even one word to cheer its loneliness, or to do one act to brighten its shadows.

"Back to the city — to the wilderness of homes.

"It was near election day.

"As we hurried on I chanced to notice a huge poster, on a board fence in a street, made poor and wretched by saloons.

"It contained these words:

'VOTE FOR SCANLAN.'

"Scanlan was the saloon-keeper. We had been finishing his work — so far as the child was concerned. Other hands had carelessly laid the father away — somewhere. It only remained for others to make the mother's grave — anywhere. It would soon be done. Then the saloon-keeper's work would be done with this family. One of one hundred.

"Perhaps he will be a councilman then — or an alderman.

"Vote for Scanlan!

"Why not? He is doing a legitimate business. He is rich. He expects to purchase absolution one day and go to the blessed company of all faithful people. The city is generous to Scanlan; it sells him a license; it gives his victims a home on the cool islands, and it digs his graves.

"'Vote for Scanlan.'"

# CHAPTER XXIV.

### THE CLIO CLUB.—AUNT'S NARRATIVE.

"We went to the Clio Club concert — husband and I.

"We were told that this was a very choice club, and that only very choice people were invited. That made me feel very choice. It is a very agreeable feeling.

"Husband was not pleased with this word 'choice' that was so freely used about the concert.

"'It neither sounds manly, democratic or American,' said he. You know what husband is — always talking about things being American.

"The programme was very choice, so everyone said. There was nothing American about that as anybody could see.

"How lovely it was — that programme, all on coffee-colored paper with rough edges! There was one piece called 'Just like Love,' marked 'Davy, Novello;' that, I thought, would be an old love song; a piano piece was printed under the name of *Presto and Canzona Napolitana; that*, I thought, would be a tune; there was a Ballade by Rheinberger, a Cantabile by Tschaikowsky, a Venetian Barcarolle, a Toccata, and a piece called 'Weinachtspastorale' and a Grand Polonaise. There was a *March et Cortege* from *La Reine de Saba;* that, I thought, would be a march; a Cavatina by Centemesi. I may not pronounce these words all quite right, but everything was foreign and far away; you see how much pains had been taken to make it choice.

"There were several ladies who assisted at the concert. These had double names, though whether they had been married several times, or whether their husbands' names were only sort of appendages, I did not know. Among them were Mrs. Smith-Scholalli and Mrs. Jones-Florence. Their names looked encouraging on the programme.

"There was a large man with a wide forehead and black hair, that sat next to husband, and a chipper little miss had a seat beside me; both were very entertainin'. The little miss informed me that the programme was very choice, and said that we were about to enjoy 'a feast of soul.' I said that as far as I could judge the programme was very promising, and that I thought *that* piece would be very grand. I pointed to the Weinachtspastorale piece, and then I whispered to husband not to let on that we had just come up from the Cape.

"I was not so very much carried away with the pieces after all. I have enjoyed hearing 'Be Kind to the Loved Ones at Home,' or ' Ben Bolt,' or the 'Old Oaken Bucket,' or the 'Old Arm-Chair,' or 'The Lake of the Dismal Swamp,' or the 'Canadian Boat Song,' quite as much as these far-away airs. The organ and piano pieces were 'wonderful,' so the little miss at my side said, but I had a great feeling of relief when they were over; and when I looked around to the clock and see how fast the time was goin', they didn't express anything to me but sound.

"'Wonderful technique,' said the little miss at my side.

"'The arithmetic of music,' said I.

"'How aptly you express it,' said she.

"'When people want inspiration, help and consolation do they go to the arithmetic?' said husband, says he.

"' If they are so educated,' said the little miss, 'they will find pleasure in intellectual music.'

"That was a very unwise remark that husband made — to that pretty girl, too. But you know what Eben is.

"About nine o'clock, when they had been playin' two pianos, and all had ended with a grand flourish and a great bobbin', and bowin', and cheerin', husband said that he wasn't 'educated up to it,' and that we had better go. He said that he wasn't much on figures. I whispered to him to sit still and not show his ignorance; that I could stand it just as long as the rest could. He seemed very restless for the last hour, husband did, and kept lookin' round at the clock.

"I *was* somewhat disappointed, after expectin' so much. If I had a-known all about the composers of these pieces, and why they wrote them, and what they were intended to signify, and from what works they were taken, and all about the arts of construction and composition of music, I would have enjoyed it. It made me feel my ignorance, especially when I noticed how much the little miss appreciated it, and how she clapped her pretty hands with delight.

"During the intermission the large man who sat by husband asked him how he enjoyed the concert. I gave him a nudge with my elbow, so he answered evasively at first.

"'There is no American music on the programme,' said he.

"'Of course not.'

"'But here are selections of music of most other nations. Have we no American composers?' said husband.

"'I never heard of any that amounted to anything,' said the large man, good-humoredly. He added: —

"'There is a strong prejudice against American music. The Clio seldom makes use of American words or music. It is very careful of its reputation; it is a very choice club. I like American art myself.'

"'But we have an American literature that the world reads; we have young American art clubs; is there no school for the development of American music; for the setting of the poetry of American life, history and scenery to song?' said husband.

"'Other nations have such clubs and schools, and are proud of their own songs, music and words. Every stream and river, and mountain and valley, has its song, and the best singers are not ashamed to sing them. We sing them. Would it not be well to have some of our own?'

"'I never heard of such a thing before. It does seem reasonable, as I think of it. It is held to be one of the fine arts, here, to be as obscure as possible; we seek to use unknown places from unknown names, as far as we can. See what a programme *that* is, for example. We prefer Italian words to German, and German to English, though old English words will do,' said he.

"He laughed as though he half agreed with husband after all.

"'But does the Club never present original compositions?'

"'Yes. Herbert once wrote a boat song on the Volga; it was received with tremendous enthusiasm.'

"'Was it published?' asked husband.

"'Yes.'

"'Did it sell?'

"'He sold enough copies to his own pupils to pay for the plates. *They* all do that.'

"He laughed again, as though it looked to him rather ridiculous.

"'Would not a song on the Charles, or Hudson, or Ohio, have been as acceptable? It would at least have been American.'

"'Perhaps so; but the days of "Hail Columbia,"

and the "Blue Juniata," are gone, and foreign teachers have taught us that the *world* is the province of music, and that music is not provincial. Every teacher teaches the music and songs of his own land; the songs that are most pleasing to him; it is only natural. The city is full of foreign music-teachers, and each is true to the music and traditions of his own country. These teachers are a great help to us, but each teaches his own art.'

"'And so the only people who are untrue to the music and traditions of their own country are Americans?' said husband.

"'So it would seem. I never knew any one except a Jenny Lind, Parepa-Rosa or a Nilsson that even dared to face a Boston audience at a concert like this with an American song. No *man* ever does. America is new. Yankee Doodle-ism is dead. Even the old Handel and Haydn Society has gone by. Why, some of these young men even laugh at Handel himself.'

"'Are you acquainted with the members of the Club?' says husband.

"'Yes.'

"'Who is the first one to the right?'

"'Hobbs.'

"'What is he?'

"'A clerk.'

"'Where was he educated?'

"'He came up from the Cape.'

"'Who is the next one?'

"'Now, this is too bad: if you go to analyzing the Club in that way you will ruin its reputation. The Club takes its tone and character wholly from its teachers; just like organ-pipes that respond to another's touch.'

"'I see.'

"'They just sing.'

"'Wouldn't a school for the purpose of the development of American music be a good thing for Boston?'

"'I think it would.'

"'Democratic — utilitarian — founded on the principles of Jeremy Bentham and John Stuart Mill, that that is the best which benefits the greatest number; a school in which musical artists should retain their own names and not be ashamed of them. Artists in other nations do this. A school that should sing American words under American titles; a school that should estimate music as an influence as well as an art.'

"'I am somewhat a utilitarian. I believe, with Mill, that the greatest happiness of the greatest number should be the aim and end of all institutions. You see how that would apply to music. That would be the best music that would be most helpful and do the most good. I think we need a school like that. Germany has such schools.'

"Now what do you think? as soon as husband said 'John Stuart Mill,' that little minx of a miss looked up to me and said:—

"'What a lovely man your husband is,—I think he is just lovely. Mill was *such* a friend to women.'

"I told husband that as we were goin' home. We both said that that would make the recollection of the evenin' very pleasant, and when we got home, and Jefferson asked Uncle how he liked the concert, he just answered:—

"'It was lovely. We had good seats.'

"After all that he had said, too!"

# CHAPTER XXV.

### ELECTION DAY.

It was Election Day. November. The air was frosty, with a steely brightness. One of those days that bring a rift of warmth into the cooling season; a calm in the month of storms; a day that ripens the leaves with which the fitful gusts of the night winds have strewn the streets.

Uncle Eben was up betimes in the morning, as was his custom on Election Day. On the Cape the elections were held in the vestry of the church, and he was always there early, just as he was always punctual at the Sabbath service and at the class and conference meeting. He had been taught by his father and grandfather to regard voting as a religious duty. He had always looked upon a large part of the Pentateuch as a political book.

He read the *Advertiser* and the *Post*. They were left at the door early. Then he went out and bought the *Herald;* then he hailed a boy and bought the *Globe*. If he was not a voter in the precinct, he wished fully to understand what were the duties of the day.

At breakfast he remarked that it was "a bright day for the election." Eugene came in and he asked him if the "prospects were bright."

"For the base-ball match? I think so. We shall have them to-day."

"For the election?"

"Election Day, is it? What for?"

Uncle looked unhappy. Said something about De Tocqueville and Mill; something about the principles of the "founders of the Republic."

Eugene was not greatly interested.

"I suppose everybody goes to town-meeting down on the Cape," said he, "Americans just the same as the foreigners? Young men just like old men — even those who do not expect an office. They have time for such things."

Eugene bustled about, making preparations for the base-ball match.

"You vote before you go out of town?" said Uncle.

"Vote? I *never* have voted. Young gentlemen do not vote. They do not want vulgar offices if they could have them."

He bustled about as before.

Uncle looked puzzled at Eugene's views of politics, but a philosophical calm came into his face after a brief disturbance.

"In this country," said he, "we have nothing but the virtue of the people to sustain our institutions and to continue them to others. The virtue of the people can only be maintained by intelligence at the polls. As long as Rome sustained her virtue she stood against the world; when she surrendered her virtue she lost her rights, and the barbarians of the North swept down and crushed her. When the Republic of Venice "—

But Uncle's audience had gone — Eugene; I was not a voter.

Uncle went to the polls early to see the descendants of the Franklins, Adamses, Otises, Sumners and Phililpses maintain the trusts of their illustrious and democratic ancestors.

The ward-room was in a public school building. This seemed fitting to Uncle; as appropriate as the church vestry. On the Cape, the church, the school and the ballot were alike sacred in his view; each belonged to the other.

The street was sentinelled with a row of patriots of various nationalities and colors; in the latter respect, red was the predominating hue. These offered ballots to the voters as they passed.

Uncle was not impressed by any very evident intelligence of these super-serviceable servants of the public.

"Never mind," said he, quietly. "This is a free country." Then, quoting John A. Andrew, he added, "'I know not what record of sin awaits me in another world, but this I do know: I never yet despised a man because he was poor, because he was ignorant, or because he was black.'"

He stopped and read the "voting-list" pasted on a fence. He noticed there the names of the ministers in the ward, the teachers, and of several merchants who had called to inquire about father, and whom Uncle had met; also, of the Browning Club, composed mostly of the sons of those merchants living on the avenue.

On the Cape the ministers voted early; the teachers at noon, and the members of the Farmers Club in the afternoon, the vote of the latter being generally unanimous and decisive.

Uncle went into the ward-room. The school furniture had been removed; there were sums and geometrical figures on the blackboards, and the floor was covered with saw-dust. Just why the halls of the patriots should have been covered with saw-dust, like a stable, Uncle was puzzled to divine.

A policeman, one of those guardians of the peace who bring to their duties a very recent knowledge of the institutions of foreign lands, offered Uncle one of the two only chairs "outside of the rail," and he gladly accepted it, and sat down in the temple of learning, to see an exhibition of patriotic interest that should prophesy of municipal greatness and glory for the centuries to come.

The ministers did not arrive.

The saloon-keepers of one of the back streets came early. They voted. They labored with their friends. They were generous; their language, if not choice, was persuasive and forcible.

The teachers did not appear.

The janitor of one of the schools came, and inquired for a ticket that contained the name Dennis Flarity, and having complimented Dennis, he retired to Dennis' emporium in the single back-alley of the ward of wealth and culture. One such back-alley, at least, is to be found in even the South End and Highland wards.

Neither did the members of the Browning Club appear; not even to give the decisive vote.

The idlers on the Square, whom Uncle had seen sunning themselves in the warm October days, came. They lingered long, and before night Uncle was able to see the utility of the saw-dust; the problem could not have been made more clear.

The day passed.

A middle-aged man of the prevailing color, who had been in the ward-room all day, seemingly a self-appointed inspector, came to Uncle with a smiling face.

"Are you a Republican or Democrat?"

"I would give," said Uncle, "to man his birthright" —

"That's the talk," said the super-serviceable patriot.

"And to labor in a field for manly independence" —

"You 're the boy," encouragingly.

"And to him that works his dues. But" —

"Ye's a gentleman. And now I will tell you in confidence that Hibberdy and Hobberdy and Smart are elected, sure. There haven't many Americans voted to-day. They are all down town, attendin' to their business. It has been a good day for us, sure."

"Who are Hibberdy and Hobberdy and Smart?"

"Merchants, sure."

"What do they deal in?"

"Importers; don't you know Hibberdy and Hobberdy?"

"What do they import?"

"Ah, my boy, they import; and, sure, they import what gives the boys the inspiration to labor, and helps build the railroads, and makes ye men what speculates rich as the princes of the ould country and the good ould times. That is a true word ye said about labor and freedom, and now I will go down to Hibberdy and Hobberdy's and congratulate. And won't ye go too?"

Uncle came back philosophically. The wind scattered the leaves over the street. There was November weather in his spirit. He said at the supper table:

> "Ill fares the land, to hastening ills a prey,
> Where wealth accumulates and men decay."

"Has any one here voted to-day?" he asked of me.

"Only Nolan."

"Nolan?"

"The coachman."

"And Neversink."

"Neversink?"

"The German girl's beau. We give him odd jobs."

It *had* been a good day for Hibberdy and Hobberdy and Smart.

# CHAPTER XXVI.

### THE LECTURESHIP. — SNOW.

"Brother Henry continued to improve, but he was still very restless, and was not willin' that we should return to the Cape.

"We went to the Lectureship — husband and I.

"I expected to see the sun, but I didn't get a ray of light — it was just like a voyage to the clouds. I had thought to receive great comfort from the Lectureship when I should come up from the Cape.

"What a scene it was! We went early, at eleven o'clock, so as to get a seat. The doors of the Temple were full; people were runnin' to and fro like boys after a cry of fire. We rushed on with the tide up one of the twenty stairways.

"It was not a sunny room. It was sort of shadowy and mysterious. There were gas-lights flashin' on a gray and gold ceiling; an organ lookin' cramped for room; dust; and people hurryin'.

"Everybody seemed movin' about; Sunday school teachers, day school teachers, young women in gray, widders in black, ministers in white neck-ties, editors, professors, literary folks, business men, clerks.

"The Temple soon filled, the aisles and the doors.

"They were honest-lookin' folks, and very intelligent, but somehow they didn't seem satisfied and contented and happy. There was a restlessness everywhere. It was not like an old Quaker meetin' at all, where people with blessed faces just said nothin', but looked serene; nor like an old-time Methodist meetin', where they used to come together to talk about assurance, and shout 'Glory!' Everybody seemed a little uncertain and dissatisfied, as though there was somethin' in life that they wanted and had not been able to find.

"The platform was full of learned men. One of them made a sort of scientific prayer to the people, and then the lecturer began to explain the mysteries of theology and science.

"I never listened so to any man. I thought every minute that he was goin' to say somethin' that I could understand. He talked amazingly;

it made me greatly excited. I knew it was all about somethin' or other, but the sentences all went over my head.

"As near as I could get the sense of it, he said that everything was all correct; the world was constructed properly, as Moses had said. Things were all in harmony above the clouds. This was very comfortin'; I had thought it was so.

"Then he proceeded to explain eschatology, and how it would all be in the future ages. That was just what everyone wanted to know, and I would rather have given five dollars than not to have understood what he said. Husband seemed to drink it all in and to be powerfully interested.

"There was an old lady that sat by my side. She was dressed in black satin, and had an ear-trumpet, and she listened as though the fate of the whole human family hung upon the speaker's lips.

"When the lecture was over she said to me: —

"'Mysterious!'

"'Yes,' said I, 'very mysterious.'

"'Who was that man he said had got the eschatology?'

"'Dorner,' said I.

"'Deep?' said she.

"'Deep,' said I.

"'Why, a person that can't see that that is deep must be lackin',' said she. 'I can see that that is deep.'

"'So can I,' said I.

"We agreed.

"I watched the crowd as it melted away. The people didn't look satisfied; they didn't seem sure. I have seen more settled-lookin' people go away from a meetin' at Yarmouth, or the Vineyard, on the old camp-grounds.

"We went out on to the Common, and passed through to the Garden, and the avenue around the hill with the monument. The air was cool and bright, and the leaves were fallin' and driftin' about on the walks under the trees.

"I asked husband how he enjoyed the discourse.

"'These Boston people have a great privilege in spending their dinner-hour in hearing theological questions discussed in that way, by one who has made them a life-long study — a great privilege,' said he. 'But the real evidence of these things does not come from without, but from within. It is a matter of experience. The Gospel promise is that all who yield to the Divine Will shall "know of the doctrine." I would give more to hear a plantation negro tell his experience than to hear a theologian try to explain it. I would rather see the light than hear a lecturer try to analyze it. But the Lectureship is a grand thing; it is intelligence *about* truth.'

"We sat down on a seat near the pond. It was sunny and sheltered. Boys were sailin' their boats on the pond.

"'This is not the first Lectureship that has been given in Boston,' said husband. 'A hundred years ago a Lectureship was held on this Common under the trees. The great elm was standing then. Ten thousand people used to attend. The lecturer's philosophy was very easy to understand; it also had to do with belief and doubt. It was, " He that seeketh, findeth."

"'Men came to scoff, but their faces turned white. Doubters came for light, and it shined within. Men rejoiced in the inward evidence, and their faces were calm and bright. This world vanished; the future glowed.

"'They called him the New Light; the movement they named the New Light stir.

"'The New Light died at Newburyport. When he was dyin' he was taken to the fields to preach once more. He said: "I go to my everlasting rest. My sun of life rose, shone, and is setting. It is about to rise to shine forever." He sleeps under one of the pulpits at Newburyport.

"'The new Lectureship is good — I do not doubt its good influence, but is it better than the old?'

"The wind blew around the hill, and we rose and went on. I saw that he had not received all the light that he expected. He talks in a kind of indirect way, husband does. He is very careful of what he says, but when you know him it is not hard to understand him.

"When we were at home he looked thoughtful. Jefferson asked him about the Lectureship and its results.

"'Well,' says husband, 'my experience reminds me of what Emerson says:—

"'I am not much of an advocate for travelling,' says Emerson, 'and I observe that men run away to other countries because they are not good in their own, and run back to their own, because they pass for nothing in new places. For the most part only light characters travel. Who are you that have no task to keep you at home?'

"'I think there is a restlessness in our people, which argues want of character.'

"'The stuff of all countries is just the same. What is true anywhere is true everywhere. Let him go where he will, the traveller can only find so much beauty or worth as he carries.'

"I have heard him quote that forty times, I know it all by heart. What does it mean?

"I never liked Emerson very well. It seems as though when I hear husband quote him that he meant *me*.

"Bright days went on, Henry was not worse — only he could get no natural sleep.

"One of the servant girls who has been sick a long time had a hemorrhage — she had no friends in this country, and I wondered what would become of her. She cried all the time, and it made my heart ache for her.

"One day she came to me with a smile, and said : —

"'Dr. Cullis says he will take me — I shall have a home. He thinks he can help me.'

"We rode out to the Consumptives' Home one day, husband and I. The doctor took us over the grounds. How beautiful they were! How pure the air was there!

"'Whatever that man may believe, he is doing good,' husband says he, 'I know of nothing more unselfish than to befriend a sick man or woman who has not a friend.'

"Husband gave the Home one hundred dollars. — I would, only for my losses in Treasure Mountain.

"We went to a Catholic orphan asylum.

"'It is doing good, doing good,' husband says he. He took out his pocket-book as he was comin' away.

"'You're not goin' to give anything to help the Catholics, are you?' says I."

"'There are no Catholics in the Sermon on the Mount,' says he; 'a true heart knows nothing of sects, but only of needs. You have not understood the parable of the Samaritan.'

"Husband is becomin' broad, husband is. I hope he won't relapse. Still, I wasn't sorry to have him give somethin' for the children, because children is children, I would have given somethin' myself: only, you know, I'd been speculatin'.

"We came home from a ride to Mount Ida one day, and found brother worse.

"It was nearly December. There was snow in the air."

## CHAPTER XXVII.

#### DECEMBER.

It is ended. How still is the house and how heavy is my heart!

The lights twinkle across the dark gulf of the Public Garden, and I look out on to the darkness, and wonder at the change, and at what it will bring, and where its results will end.

The street band is playing 'Departed Days.' Light steps pass—and happy voices melt away on the air.

The doctor said that he did not expect it so soon. He knew that his nervous system was exhausted, but he thought the streams of life would flow back again from nature's mysterious sources. He was called too late.

How dark, how dreadful were those last days! His brain had not slept for weeks — it had had no rest but the stupor of the drug. Life passed into a deep horror; then memory into oblivion. He did not know us; he did not suffer at the end.

One day the cloud partly lifted. He thought

he was in the old orchard on the Cape again. He was a boy; it was spring; the trees were in bloom and the robins were singing. He was a boy, and happy, and years lay fair before him. There came a vision of life, with its ambitions and struggles, and he said : —

"Hurry, hurry — how they hurry; how the years hurry!"

I put my hand on his forehead. Tears came to his eyes, and a helpless look into his face. Then his face lighted.

"Is that your hand, mother?"

"No; Jefferson's."

"God bless you, my son. I thought it was mother's. Do not leave me. It is going — my mind is going — this is Night."

He never spoke again. He lived on, but the world seemed all lost to him. Three weeks ago it ended; at midnight.

"Insolvent." When the lawyer said that, I knew the whole truth; how the ruinous state of his business had produced the long, silent anxiety; the solitary anxiety, sleeplessness; insomnia, nervous exhaustion, and the exhaustion the collapse. His disease had begun in the over-use of his nervous resources to gain wealth and to sustain the demands of an exacting social position. He had consumed himself.

For us: for me. Poor father!

What are we to do? My step-mother is going back to her old home. Eugene is fitted for nothing useful. He is as proud as he is penniless. He says he shall join an orchestra, and travel. It looks to me like moral death. Archie has entered a dry-goods house as a clerk. Fashionable life and its habits have unfitted him for any independent occupation. Carrie and I are going to Uncle Eben's for the present. It is my purpose to go West.

To-morrow the house will be closed. The beautiful furniture will be taken away by the auctioneer; the pictures, the ornaments, the silver, all. We have given up everything to meet the demands of the law; we go out as helpless as the emigrants who land on our shores.

Friendship? How strangely we are already forgotten by those who used to share our hospitalities. The polite associations of society hardly deserve *that* name. Friends? — we seemed to have more than we could welcome — they are now reduced to two — Uncle and Aunt, on the Cape. They are true; they only.

## CHAPTER XXVIII.

#### AUNT DESIRE HEARS FROM THE WEST.

"Eben!

"Wonder of wonders: the apple trees are all bloomin' in January! Who would ever have thought that I would have lived to see a day like this?

"Eben?

"'What now?' Come here and tell me what this means.

"Let me read you this letter — from Henry: —

"'*I have been elected to Congress.*'

"To Congress! Just think o' that! I feel just as though the Lord had appeared to me in the burnin' bush. I always told ye, Eben, that the sons of these old Cape families turned out well — now, didn't I? Good stock, well brought up; have some principles and character to put into life. There's nothin' better to make a man of than an old-fashioned New England character, with a little Calvinism thrown in, though I am a Methodist who say it.

"'*My majority was over three thousand, which is one thousand more than usual party strength, and expresses the public confidence in my character, and this expression gives me more satisfaction than the mere fact of my election.*'

"That is good. I always tried to bring Henry up to respect himself. I always told him that whoever's respect he might lose, never to lose the respect of Henry Endicott. Won't I be proud to put his name on my family tree!

"'*Brother John has been made president of the Western Home Mission Society and is engaged in establishing new schools and churches in Dakota, and in the region of the Red River Valley of the North. He has already commenced some twenty schools and organized twelve churches.*'

"There, that reads just like a story. I always desired that one of my sons might become a lawyer and one a minister, and here I am blessed with more than I ever asked for. I have always heard that the good wishes of the mother turn into realities in the children.

"'*I owe my apparent success much to your influence, and as greatly to father's sound opinions and excellent example.*'

"'Sound opinions,' 'excellent example.' So you are somebody, Eben, after all! I'm glad. I wish I'd found it out before; it would have saved me from some hard feelin's, and so much talk, you know. But we can't always see the end from the beginning.'

"'I'm satisfied now, Eben; everything is all right in the world, as the Lectureship said. If you are all right, the world is all right. And Eben, I'm never goin' to find fault with you any more. I don't feel as though I had always done quite right by you in the past. But life all appears to me differently now, just as the world appears when you see it from a hill-top.

"There is always somethin' to cast a shadow into the sunniest day — Carrie is feelin' bad, She has had a disappointment — Rev. Mr. Glass.

"He says as how he has no means of support, and she has none, and as how he does not receive a 'call,' and she has not been brought up to economy, he can only be a *sister* to her — I think he meant a brother. He says as how the world is progressin', but hasn't yet reached his standard of thought.

"How brother's family have gone to pieces! Their house gone, and their furniture sold under the hammer. Eugene a fiddler, and Archie a clerk in a dry-goods store. Carrie is a good girl, a girl of talent, but so dependent and unhappy.

"The fact is that that family had wrong views of life, now didn't they? Their father gave his heart to wealth, and their step-mother to society, and there's somethin' in life better than that, now ain't there? Oaks don't grow from sun-flower seeds. What's that? '*I've arrived at these views rather late in life?*' Yes, Eben, but since the Lord has blessed us so greatly, you'll forgive me, now won't ye? You know what I am, you know. Don't you never say nothin'."

# CHAPTER XXIX.

### MAY — THE PRESIDENT'S LEVEE — LIFE LIES FAIR BEFORE ME.

It is May. The lilacs have budded, and the blue-birds and orioles are flitting among the apple-blossoms. The sky, stretching over the Bay, is serene and blue.

I am at Uncle Eben's.

A year and a half has passed away since the great changes in our family. Since that dreadful December. I have been at Uncle's since those dark days.

I have changed. My views of life, my hopes and aims are not what they were, and not what might be expected of a young man schooled in society. I am about to marry the daughter of a worthy Cape farmer, and am going West: into the valley of the Dakota River to begin life with my wife in a new town.

Eugene and Archie ridicule my decision and purpose. Eugene still plays in the orchestra; he has a dissipated look that troubles me; he fiddles for fifteen dollars a week and calls it *art*. I could not do that after living so long under the influence of Uncle Eben; Eugene avoids Uncle; he does not visit him or write to him.

Archie is at Meade and Meadow's. He gets eight dollars a week. He lives in a cheap boarding house; boasts that if he is poor he is still *proud*. He never speaks of Uncle. I know that Uncle would be glad to help him if he were to show the right spirit, and I see that he is just such an adviser as he needs. But Archie is in sympathy with the social views and habits of Eugene, and puts himself wholly under his influence.

Since Mr. Glass broke his engagement with her, Carrie has lived with Uncle and his family. She is now at Washington, with cousin Henry. She is to be married in June.

I have read much since I have lived at Uncle's. In politics, I have been much influenced by the principles of Jeremy Bentham, and in social opinions, by John Stuart Mill. But while I reverence the democracy of Mill, I can not respect his religious views. I accept the principle that the happiness of the greatest number should be the aim and end of all institutions; but I find the same doctrine set forth in the Sermon on the Mount, and in the Gospel Parables, and made clear in Paul's argument in Corinthians; and I have come to the conclusion that the habits, aims, and hopes of a religious life are essential to the happiness of men. In short, I have come to believe what Uncle has often said to me, "that no one can be perfectly happy unless he believes that the door of Heaven stands open to him at the end of life."

I saw three things in human experience that impressed me as fundamental: that all virtue is rewarded, that all evil is punished, and that the spiritual life set forth in the Scriptures is the hightest good of the soul and the completion of its happiness. These views so influenced me that I have consecrated my life, and have entered into the joys of a religious experience, and united with the little Methodist Church in the village.

I know but little of the ecclesiastical machinery used by John Wesley and his followers, whom I merely believe to have been good men. I look upon this church as merely one of the many spiritual orders of equal value, but especially adapted to pioneer work in the West, where its fruits have been good.

Uncle knew that I was thinking earnestly on these subjects, and he was more than pleased at my conclusions. He used to say, "Be not deceived; cast your anchor, my boy, into ground that will hold."

So a Jeffersonian Democrat in politics, evangelical in religion, and the husband of a true-hearted, sensible, country wife, I expect to go West. I have aimed to "cast anchor into ground that will hold." I feel the certainty of usefulness, and success within me.

Aunt has not spoken an unpleasant or censorious word to uncle since she returned from that sad visit to the city. Uncle and aunt have had but one difficulty since that experience; that was about the making of their will.

They consulted "the boys," John and Henry, about the matter. John wrote that he did not wish for any part of their property, as he had already enough of his own. He said, "Give it all to Henry."

Henry answered, "Give it all to John. I am well enough off. I do not need it."

"How much does a young man need to make a fair start in the West?" asked aunt, after the last letter had been received.

"A thousand dollars," said uncle.

"Let us give Jeff a thousand dollars."

"Yes; that is what we must do," said uncle.

"And don't let us wait until we are dead, let us give it to him now," said aunt. "We shall never miss it."

"That is just what we will do," said Uncle. "That is just my plan, I agree with you exactly."

"One can't do much in distributin' property after one is dead," said Aunt.

Uncle was of the same opinion.

"Now let us will all the rest to the Woman's Board."

"To the American Board, you mean?"

"No, to the Woman's Board;" and Aunt proceeded to deliver a missionary address as would have astonished by its array of facts a professor in history. Uncle was firm.

The discussion went on for several days, when it was decided to give half of the estate to the Old Men's Home and the Old Women's Home, and to divide the other half equally between the two Boards. After that Uncle and Aunt both returned to their former social state of serenity and happiness.

Last winter Uncle and Aunt visited Washington,

at the invitation of Cousin Henry. Carrie and I managed the old place while they were gone. I think from what he wrote me, that nothing ever gave Cousin Henry so much honest pride as to receive his father and mother and entertain them at the Capital.

"Jefferson," said Aunt Desire, on her return, "what do you think? He took me to the President's reception, and all these grand people treated me like a queen. The dress I wore cost two hundred dollars — Henry paid for it. Think of it, Jeff — two hundred dollars — I didn't feel right — I felt as though my stone-colored silk would have done just as well, and that the money ought to have been saved and have been given to the Woman's Board. Henry did not mean I should know how much that dress did cost, but the dressmaker by mistake sent the bill to me. When I saw it I was that overcome that I held my breath, but Henry said it was right."

Dear Aunt Desire: Her hobby is the Woman's Board. Why should it not be? It makes her happy; it makes her feel that she has a mission, and that her life has been an especial value among the factors of the world.

I am sorry to leave the dear old house on the

AT THE PRESIDENT'S RECEPTION.

Cape; its orchard; the meadows; the graveyard where my ancestors lie; Pine Tree Hill. But I go to carry all the good I have learned at Uncle Eben's into a new town in a new country, and this life, and a life beyond this life, lie fair before me, and I am a happy man.

Since Uncle and Aunt have settled their affairs for life, Uncle has seemed to be in a frame of mind truly patriarchal.

He said to me one day —

"My land journey is over. I am waiting by the shore for the sail that shall take me beyond the horizon. I have ate from many a table, but I have hungered again. I have drank from many a fountain, but I thirsted again. Better things are beyond — beyond. I am willing that the tent should fall. I have a home that will last."

He goes to the simple church under the hill; to the place of graves. He is not quite seventy, but he feels that he has already reached the border of the new country, and that his work is done.

Life lies serene behind him. It is bright above him and before him. Would that the world were richer in simple lives like his! I am assured that I shall part from the man whose influence made me when I shall take his hand to say farewell.

Aunt sees the change.

"He grows better and better every day. You know what husband is, you know."

"Yes, we all know that."

www.ingramcontent.com/pod-product-compliance
Lightning Source LLC
Chambersburg PA
CBHW032005230426
43672CB00010B/2251